More Than Meets the Eye

True stories about Death, Dying and Afterlife

By Yvonne Perry

More Than Meets the Eye
True Stories About Death, Dying and Afterlife
Yvonne Perry
ISBN 0-9753870-8-1
Copyright © 2004

Published by:
Nashville, TN 37214
615-415-9861

To purchase copies of this book please visit
www.yvonneperry.net

Cover photos courtesy of Kevin Britland, Norman Pogson, Jenny Solomon via Dreamstime.com and Freestockphotos.com.

Acknowledgements

When my college instructor, Gary Kuhn, first encouraged me to write about transitioning to the Afterlife I laughed it off thinking I was unqualified to write about the topic. When I mentioned to a friend that I was ghostwriting a book for someone else, he asked me, "Why don't you write a book of your own?" My response was, "What would I write about?" I thought no more about it until Linda Woods said, "Yvonne, you ought to write a book about spirit guides—you are always in touch with someone from the Other Side!" The light bulb went on, I connected the dots, and the inspiration to write this book began in earnest.

I thank the wonderful people who shared their experiences with me. I have gained much insight by looking at death and afterlife through your eyes. Thank you to those souls in the non-physical realm, for allowing me to tell your story. You have taught me so much!

Blessings to K'lynn Ragsdale, Wanda Snell, Randy Perry, Terry Emge, Juliet Nightingale and my own dear mother, Doris Mauldin, who diligently proofread this book. A special thanks to Linda Woods, who edited and edited and edited, and kept me encouraged with her enthusiasm. Because of you, the readers will have a much easier time understanding what I meant to write! My appreciation goes to Juliet Nightingale for writing such an eloquent foreword.

I would also like to thank my husband, Randy Perry, for his patience, encouragement and support during the many hours I have spent at the computer while writing this book.

About The Author

Yvonne Perry is a freelance writer and public speaker, who has also authored and self-published *Email Episodes: A Hilarious Look at Life*, and five children's books. She is a graduate of American Institute of Holistic Theology where she earned a Bachelor of Science in Metaphysics. She enjoys researching and writing about science, healing and spirituality. Yvonne is married to Randy Perry and is the mother of two children, stepmother of three, and grandmother of six.

Yvonne is available as a keynote speaker to present the subject of any of her books at your event. For more information please see *www.yvonneperry.net* or call 615-415-9861.

A person starts to live when he can live outside himself. Few are those who see with their own eyes and feel with their own hearts.

— Albert Einstein

Table of Contents

Preface

I wrote this book to help people prepare for a peaceful and successful transition, to alleviate the fear associated with the dying process and to remind us to make the most of our very precious lives.

Although I have had a few "close calls" with death, I do not a consider myself to be an expert in the field of dying or afterlife research. However, I have always been intrigued by the mystery of crossing over to the Other Side. As a child it was common for my parents to take me with them to Lownde's Funeral Home when someone from our church died. The experience did not upset me. In fact, I actually enjoyed trying to read the cursive writing on those tiny cards tucked between the mums and roses! I felt peaceful with the soft music and floral-scented atmosphere as I pretended to be Goldilocks trying out all the different chairs in the parlor. I can remember sitting in church and listening to the preacher talk about Heaven. *If Heaven is so wonderful*, I reasoned in my young mind, *why are people so sad when someone dies and goes there?* As a young adult, I watched my family deal with our own critically ill loved ones, and was again puzzled by their hesitancy to let them go. As an adult, I enjoy strolling through old cemeteries and reading the headstones of the dearly departed. I daydream about what each person was like while living and wonder what they are doing in the Afterlife or if they have returned for another stint on Earth. These experiences and my desire to help others overcome their fear of death have been a catalyst for writing this book. *More Than Meets the Eye* is not an authority on death and afterlife. It is simply a collection of stories people have shared with me, as well as a few of my own observations, opinions and experiences thrown in for good measure.

Some who read this book may soon be preparing for a transition to the Afterlife. Others may be caregivers, friends or family of a critically ill patient who is near the end of this life, or has recently passed. Others may have experienced a close brush with death and then lived to tell about it. I am indeed grateful to the people who shared their experience with me during the writing of this book. I trust that the stories will offer hope and yes, even excitement, when you help a loved one pass, or when you face your own transition.

> Oh death where is thy sting.
> Oh, grave where is thy victory?

Foreword

When we were in Chicago at our IANDS (*International Association for Near-Death Studies*) annual conference in June 2004, I was speaking with PMH Atwater—a noted author, researcher and speaker on the near-death phenomenon—who told me that it was God's will for me to be back in Nashville—that I had very special work to do centered on the near-death experience (NDE) that would reach people far and wide. I had recently returned to Nashville, but was uncertain as to why I was called back—having left Nashville to return to the northeast to be with my daughter, so that we could be closer to each other. I'd thought that my time in Nashville was complete—that my mission had been accomplished and that I'd not return. I've since given it the analogy that returning to Nashville was like having an NDE; I had to come back to fulfill a special mission...

I started a local Friends of IANDS (FOI) discussion/support group in Nashville in 2002, but it was a very small group. That being the case, I didn't think that I would be needed again in Nashville, once I had left—especially since there appeared to be little interest in the NDE or any real need for support at the time, or so I had thought. At this point my whole life had become a vocation centered on the NDE and similar experiences, death, dying, the Afterlife and the immortality of the soul. One of the main reasons I was sent back from the Other Side, time and time again, was to proclaim the truth that, indeed, we live forever! This was no longer a theory for me; it was *fact*, because I've *been* there, as have countless others.

Upon returning to Nashville I did re-establish the FOI and found, to my delight, that more and more people were showing interest and attending the meetings! At our meeting on 14 June, 2004, WSMV Channel 4 News appeared and put us on the news that very night! This happened after having only been back in Nashville for two months!

More and more people started attending our FOIs and what a treasure trove of individuals they've been indeed! People who'd had near-death, out-of-body and other spiritually transformative experiences were present—very talented people, including Yvonne Perry, who were currently working on, or who have written books or produced films, art and music—all inspired by NDEs, OBEs & STEs! Look at all of these extraordinary people!—I thought. I've since come to find out that Nashville is *loaded* with experiencers—experiencers from all walks of life and backgrounds—all sitting here together and openly sharing from their hearts. We've shared stories of our experiences, questions, insights, laughter and tears ... and I was so moved I could hardly contain myself. The 'Love vibe' was everywhere! I felt gratitude in the deepest respect. Something special was, indeed, unfolding right before my very eyes and I've never failed to be in total awe.

While back in the northeast, I became the Membership Chair for IANDS and was very busy encouraging NDErs and other interested individuals to join IANDS—the premier global organization for experiencers, researchers, health care providers, etc. that provides support, resources and amity with kindred spirits. As one who'd been silent about my NDEs for so many years, I was utterly elated to find out about such an organization being in existence and that I could now connect with other experiencers all over the world and gain access to resources that would help me in ways I never could have imagined! Being a member of IANDS, and particularly facilitating a support group, has afforded me the opportunity to compare notes with other experiencers and for all of us to be reassured that, indeed, we are *not* crazy! We've had experiences that, undeniably, change and transform our lives forever—experiences that, in many cases, have enabled us to tap into and remember who we *really* are! We've also been able to experience direct communion with the Light Source, or All That Is—as well as other spirit beings—and to know, firsthand, what *unconditional love* is. Now what, pray tell me, can be "crazy" about that? Personally, I cannot think of anything more liberating or validating! This, to me, is the real meaning of being "born again"—a term so misconstrued by Christian fundamentalists!

For so many years, experiencers have been "in the closet" about their having had an NDE or similar experience for fear of being misunderstood, judged, ridiculed or even persecuted. Some experiencers have ended up in a mental ward or put on drugs ... and some child experiencers being slapped and shouted at and silenced by a parent or other relative, because of the prevailing ignorance surrounding the NDE! It was rare to see anything featured in mainstream media about NDEs—least of all in broadcast media. People just didn't talk about it. In fact, I didn't even know about IANDS until 1997 nor was I even aware of Dr. Raymond Moody, who coined the term 'near-death experience'. Yet IANDS has been in existence since the early 1980s! So one can see why so many of us have remained hidden—more for the sake of self preservation—and trying to lead as normal a life as possible. Therefore, in order to avoid persecution or being "excommunicated", as it were, we fell into silence...

Now, the NDE is not only being openly talked about, it's receiving widespread media interest—in both print and broadcast media—everywhere across the globe. You'll see NDE-related material all over the place and it's even become a household term! In recent years, even I have been featured in various print media as well as having been on radio and now TV! There's nowadays a wealth of material, resources, support and individuals right within reach—including right here in Nashville! On a daily basis, I receive emails from around the world—all from individuals who are interested in or who have had an NDE (or what I prefer to call an *Eternal Life Experience, ELE*).

Not only that, but the whole issue of death had remained such a stigma—something you just didn't talk or even hardly think about—something that was utterly taboo! There are countless individuals in our world who are still terrified of death. Why? Because they think that that's the *end*---end of the story. Poof! That's it! You're gone forever! Nothing could be further from the truth and that's why so many of us have been sent back from the Other Side—to *affirm* that *life is eternal* and that we *do* carry on ... as conscious, living, thriving beings with incredible power and love!

With a subject that had been silent and hidden for so long—now emerging into the light of day, imagine, then, the joy that I felt when I was approached by Yvonne Perry, who was writing a book on death, dying and the Afterlife. I was only too pleased to work with her—the FOI also proving to be a magnificent source for material and support from other NDErs in this special project. It is time for the taboo to be broken. It is time for all of the lies and fear about death to be abolished once and for all! And it is individuals like Yvonne Perry who are truly helping to accomplish this great task. Yvonne has done such a splendid job in bringing forth such vital and pertinent information that covers all facets of death, dying and the Afterlife—a subject that must be faced squarely in order to free us of the illusions and fear that have plagued us throughout human history.

Returning to Nashville and being a conduit for generating support for and a community of people who've had near-death and similar experiences has proved invaluable, indeed. This is a special time that we've just entered into. It's time for our *coming out*—coming "out of the closet" as NDErs ... because it is safe now to do so. It is time that we, as experiencers, are no longer an invisible, silent minority. Alas, for every NDEr who's come forth and spoken out about his or her NDE, there are the same number—if not more—who have yet to boldly come forth and declare , "I, too, have had an NDE!"

There is a Bulgarian proverb that states: "*At birth we cry. At death we understand why*". The book that you are about to read will provide loving and clear insight into the meaning of this profound statement. As you read these pages, you will begin to experience a sense of what it is like to be truly liberated and free—as a bird that's suddenly freed of its cage and allowed to fly. This book is a real page-turner that is so lovingly conveyed in a language that's easy to understand. It is empowering and uplifting material that will leave you no longer in a state of doubt or fear. Outside of having an NDE or similar experience yourself, these pages will bring forth wisdom, hope and a profound peace of mind.

Rev. Juliet Nightingale

Introduction

There are many commonly held views regarding death and the existence of an afterlife. Some Westernized Americans view death as a fearful tragedy, the end of a life, a sad finality. Most view it as a separation between the physical and non-physical realms. In contrast, the Ancients grieved when a baby was born and rejoiced when someone died. Regardless of our religion or culture, most of us are curious about where we came from, and what our existence after death might hold.

Our physical body is not who we are. It is only the container or vehicle for our soul. When we see someone riding a bus we know that they still exist even when they get off. It's the same with us. We exist regardless of whether we have a physical body or not. Like photosensitive eyeglasses that turn dark in the sun or transparent in the dark, a soul may choose to alter its expression or change its appearance in order to better suit its needs. Removing the limitations of a gravity-bound human body allows the soul to travel in spirit form and complete tasks in another dimension. Be assured that if your loved one has passed on, they are in spirit form and they have work to do in other worlds and realms. They are likely to be near you even though you may be unaware of their presence.

I was raised in a Southern Baptist home and continued in a fundamental religion until I was forty years old. You may be wondering how someone who was raised in such a dogmatic environment ever came to believe in reincarnation. I have to admit I was adamantly opposed to the idea when a friend of mine first mentioned it. She recommended a book by Elizabeth Clare Prophet entitled *Reincarnation: The missing Link in Christianity*. After reading the book, I saw with new eyes, the many references to reincarnation throughout the Bible and became even more curious. I began researching and found more information that seems to indicate that we are eternal souls with ongoing missions; that time exists only on earth; and that everything is happening simultaneously. It dawned on me that being in human form is only one way we progress spiritually on our path back to our Creator.

As most people do, I've always believed in angels. As a child, I interacted with what is often believed to be "imaginary playmates" and thought nothing strange of it. As a teenager, I continued to be a spiritual seeker, but as I became an adult, my curiosity and openness to the spirit world caused me to feel like a misfit. Questioning the dogma and legalistic practices dictated by the clergy, I was cast out of several churches that adhered to a rigid, traditional belief system. I finally realized that I was never going to fit into a mainstream denomination. Against my first husband's approval, and in spite of his fearful warnings about what I might be getting into, I began attending churches that were more accepting of spiritual phenomenon. A few years after being "baptized in the Holy Spirit" in a Pentecostal church, my ability to sense the presence of an angel or spirit increased. At times, I was afraid of what I was experiencing and thought that maybe these were the "demons" my religious instruction had warned me about—or perhaps I was going crazy! The church I was attending taught spiritual warfare tactics, so I began doing battle with these entities, using Bible scripture and commanding them to leave me or other people alone! All the while, day visions and night dreams were becoming more conversational and involved more loving beings who had no intent to harm me. I started listening more and battling less.

In 1988, my grandfather died. He began coming to me in my dreams and sharing his experience in the Afterlife. He even gave me helpful advice regarding a problem I was having with my daughter. I followed his advice and the problem was quickly solved. In 2000, my life fell apart and I began to challenge the belief system I had held. I began researching church history and other religions. I explored other spiritual paths to see what they had to say about spirits, angels and afterlife. Slowly, I learned to trust my inner guidance and as a result, I embraced a more compassionate approach to dealing with the deceased spirits who kept finding their way to me. Many were afraid and confused souls. Now I know they wanted help in finding the Light of God and crossing over to the Other Side.

After I read Sylvia Browne's book, *Past Lives, Future Healing*, I knew reincarnation was not only possible, but that the theory of cellular memory was very credible. After having a past-life regression with a *Karma Releasing* audio tape by Doreen Virtue, I was convinced that I had lived many times on earth. Today, I never doubt it. Memory of my past lives actually helped me resolve some unfinished business and clarify my present journey.

The point of this book is not to persuade you that one way is correct or incorrect, or to create a new doctrine, but rather to offer information and insight that may assist you in creating your own beliefs about this mysterious process of transitioning back to God/Source. Many people refuse to consider any explanation that doesn't match the viewpoints they already own. If you are convinced ahead of time (like I was years ago) that something is or isn't true, you will be tempted to find data that substantiates your belief. Therefore, I encourage you to keep an open mind and consider the ideas presented in this book as if you were in your car, curiously trying out a new road to see where it might lead. You may find that it brings you to a new or better understanding of death and afterlife. You may discover a road less traveled, and realize it was running parallel to your familiar route all along. Perhaps you, too, will see more than meets the eye.

Crossover

Silence fills the room,
Except for the soft turbulent sound of fluid filling
tubes,

There is life in the room,
But it is not the life given by
Machines and pumps,

It is life given by the Life-Giver
By the spirit within which reaches out in response
to love words spoken to comfort,
To calm the fear that stalks relentlessly about.

It is Life at it's finest,
Conquering the last enemy
Spirit joined to Spirit
Completing the circle.

— Mary Anne Womack

Chapter One: Fear of the Unknown

Screaming, moaning, groaning, and sorrowful sobs could be heard from the medical intensive care unit of Vanderbilt University Medical Center all the way down the corridor on the seventh floor. The ventilator had just been turned off for a young woman who was dying of AIDS. The woman never took a breath once the support was removed. She passed immediately and without a struggle. However, the family completely fell apart emotionally and were not prepared to accept the passing of their loved one with any amount of understanding or peace. In contrast, Terry Emge shares her story:

Upon arrival, I found Mother in her chair. Her respirations were agonal, her pupils were fixed and dilated and she had a strong steady pulse. I asked my grandmother, who was ninety-one, what had happened and she said, "Virginia grabbed the back of her head and said, 'Get Terry.' Those were the last words she spoke.

Despite my efforts at resuscitation and my medical background (I am an RN, CRNFA for a busy cardiac surgical practice), I knew in my heart that she had come to the end of her life on earth.

A definitive diagnosis was made by CT scan. She had suffered a massive hemorrhagic stroke. Our options were to temporarily monitor her in ICU on a ventilator or make a decision to withdraw life support. Her chances of survival were minimal at best.

After a discussion with her physicians and caregivers, it was decided to withdraw life support. During all of this, my mother's condition remained unchanged—fixed, dilated pupils, strong pulse, and normal blood pressure. Her ventilator was disconnected and her pulse and blood pressure remained stable.

The hospital chaplain student that was with me, my husband and best friend, Diane said to me, "Sometimes you have to tell them it's okay to go." As I was holding my mother's hand, I kissed her, told her that I loved her and that I would take care of Mom-Mom and for her to go to the Light. Within five minutes, her pulse and blood pressure slowed and her spirit went to be with God.

My mother had had a near-death experience earlier in her life. When my brother was born in 1952, she had a post-partum hemorrhage. She relayed to me that she had walked through a misty grey valley and was aware of relatives that had died when she was a child. She was drawn to the Light, the brightest and most pure she had ever seen and she had a sense of "utter peace". Her only thought was of how beautiful it was there and how she longed to remain, but she knew she had two small children to care for. Suddenly a voice like thunder said, "Ye shall live." She awoke in her hospital *bed and began to realize what she had experienced. From that moment in her life she was not afraid to die.*

As I stood beside her stretcher in the ER, knowing there was no chance for her survival, but not yet wanting her to leave me or those who loved her here on earth, I felt a sense of peace. Mother was not afraid to die—she had reassured me of that "beautiful, wondrous place" and I knew she was finally in heaven.

Some families are able to let go and even assist their loved one in transitioning. Why do some families or cultures process death so differently than others? Perhaps the fear of the unknown is what makes death so intimidating. If only we knew what was on the Other Side. Is there an afterlife or not? Do our deceased loved ones live in another dimension or reality? Are they near us? Can they see or hear us? Knowing for sure what lies ahead might make a difference in how we handle death.

Much of what we believe about death and dying is taught to us by religious doctrine. Our main attitudes about death and afterlife are deeply connected with our religious beliefs which may either confuse or comfort us. For example, if someone believes in a legalistic or angry God that punishes for sin, then death for that person may be frightening. If someone believes that we all go to a better place after death, regardless of our earthly behavior, that person may not have as many concerns about dying.

> FEAR is the chariot in which man rides to death; And when he finds himself within the chamber of the dead, he learns that he has been deceived ~ his chariot was a myth, and death a fancy child.
>
> — Levi / Aquarian Gospel

There is a huge difference between Eastern and Western cultural views on death; specifically about beliefs in salvation, reincarnation, and the afterlife. Buddhism, Hinduism and other Eastern religions believe in a progression of the soul after death. These philosophies teach that an accumulation of bad or good karma affects rebirth into either a favorable or unfavorable situation. Western religions tend to look at the present life as a one-and-only chance to "get it right" with the end result being an eternity in either Heaven or Hell. Most Catholics believe in an interim state called Purgatory where those who are borderline between deserving Heaven or Hell work their way up. Jewish beliefs most often do not include the typical Christian idea of an eternal hell. Jewish people see hell as a separation from God rather than an actual place of fire and brimstone. Therefore, Heaven may be considered as a reuniting with God's light or spirit and not necessarily as a physical place with streets of gold as many Christians believe. The Aramaic word for death is interpreted "not here, present elsewhere" and shows a belief in an afterlife. Modern day scientific studies show that there is a consciousness of mind after death and that the mind and the brain are not one in the same.

Many of our fears are rooted in delusions or distorted ways of looking at life and the world around us. Generally, our fear of death is an unrealistic fear. We tend to either ignore the subject altogether or become morbidly obsessed by it. Perhaps the best way to overcome the fear of death is to remember that our present physical life had a beginning. There was a time when we were not on Earth in these physical bodies, and there will be a time when we shall return to a non-physical state of being. The rational mind has difficulty believing that any reality other than the third dimensional world of time and space, in which we currently live, could possibly exist. We have been trained since birth to thrive in it. We know ourselves to be who we are by our external experiences; however, looking inwardly may give us a different perspective.

The sorrow, grief and sense of loss are real, but our fear about death is only an illusion. You've faced many things in life that are more frightening and unknown than death. For example, public speaking is said to be the greatest fear a person can face. So, if you've ever spoken in public then you have faced a fear said to be worse than the fear of dying. The famous comedian Jerry Seinfeld once said, "If you're at a funeral, you're better off in the casket than doing the eulogy!"

Death should be feared no more than birth, for there is no real separation between the physical and non-physical realms. The separation seems real because there is a very thin veil (i.e.: our skin and physical body) between the two realms that dims our ability to interact with those in other dimensions. But more than the physical sense of separation, we limit ourselves with the false belief that we have only five senses with which to explore and experience life. This belief hinders us from accepting what our inner knowing tells us is true. We are multi-sensory spiritual creatures able to sense the presence and energy of non-physical beings. Those who do interact with the non-physical realm are sometimes considered insane or in need of psychiatric help. Many are shunned and ridiculed. Some children are even punished for talking about seeing angels and spirits.

The Earth plane is simply another facet of our experience as souls. We are spirit beings having a human earthly experience. We all come from the same Source regardless of what we call it—God/Goddess, Spirit, Energy, Creator or whatever vocabulary term one wishes to use. Even though we manifest in individual bodies and have the illusion of separateness, there is no real division in our spirit. An ethereal mist or cloud of spirit exists where every soul is united with God and with one another. From this cloud extends a line of energy or Spirit to the Earth plane where it manifests as a suit of human flesh.

Illustration 1

Who we really are is only a small portion of what we see in each other. It is like poking your fingertip through a hole in a bed sheet draped over your body. What is hidden behind the sheet is so much greater than the fingertip—so much greater than the small portion that meets the eye!

After its mission is accomplished in the earthly realm, the soul essence simply returns to the spirit cloud to continue its work or to wait for another opportunity to manifest into human form. This return to Source may occur as a result of the body's deterioration and inability to support the soul as a vehicle and thus death of the physical body occurs. Because the soul craves authenticity, living an incongruent life may cause us to subconsciously create disease, physical deterioration, or ultimately death as a means to leave the physical body.

According to the Old Testament, humans originally had the ability to live forever. The book of Genesis teaches that death occurred for mankind as a punishment for the sin committed by Adam and Eve. Still, some Biblical characters were noted to have lived for almost a thousand years. What happened that caused our lifespan to be so shortened? In light of the technological and medical advances, it would seem that the opposite should be true. Some, like Elijah mentioned in the Bible, didn't die. Jesus took his resurrected body with him when he ascended as a light body. Living a long, healthy life requires us to live in integrity with our inner truth. It requires unplugging from belief systems that prevent us from living life to the fullest.

What we do with our life is our choice. Even dying is a choice we make! It is my belief that God does not infringe upon our free will or tell us what to do with our life. Instead, God very gently leads us to learn at our own pace, and never forces us to do anything we do not wish to. Life is the picture we paint by the decisions we make. Since a soul has choice (free will) it may simply choose to return to Source. I believe this is why we have SIDS (Sudden Infant Death Syndrome) and other unexplainable departures from a body that is otherwise healthy. The soul changes its mind about being in the physical body, or has another idea about what might best assist it on its spiritual journey. While any death causes grief for the remaining family, it is ultimately the soul's choice to move on. Free will is something we have not been taught to accept, appreciate or consciously exercise. In order to understand and accept death as a natural part of the soul's evolution, we must be able to allow people to choose for themselves on all levels. It is normal to feel anger towards God when our loved one leaves his or her physical body, but it is not God's choice. God does not take a soul against its will. The soul chooses to leave in the best interest of its evolution. We may have difficulty accepting that our loved one's death could have been a part of a greater plan—especially when it doesn't fit our expectation.

What is death? What is dying like? The best way to obtain information about death is from those who have had a first-hand experience with death; those who have died and returned to tell about it. These are referred to as near-death experiences (NDEs). P.M.H. Atwater is one of the original researchers in the field of near-death studies. In her book, *The Complete Idiot's Guide to Near-Death Experiences*, an NDE is loosely defined as an intense awareness, sense or experience of "otherworldliness", whether pleasant or unpleasant, that happens to people who are at the edge of death. It occurs for people regardless of age, education, culture or religious background. Atwater began her work in 1978 and comes from the vantage point of being a near-death experiencer—not just a mere researcher. She believes there is a step-up of energy at the moment of death, an increase in speed as if you are suddenly vibrating faster than before. Using radio as an analogy, this speed-up is comparable to having lived all your life at a certain radio frequency and then someone or something comes along and flips the dial. That flip of the dial shifts you to another, higher wavelength. The original frequency is still there as it was before. Only you changed. You sped up to allow entry into the next radio frequency. As is true with all radios and radio stations, there can be bleed-over or distortion of transmission signals due to interference patterns. These can allow or force frequencies to coexist or commingle for indefinite periods of time. Normally, most shifts on the dial are fast and efficient, but occasionally, one can run into interference, perhaps from a strong emotion, a sense of duty, or a need to fulfill a vow or keep a promise. This interference could allow coexistence of frequencies for a few seconds, days, or even years (perhaps explaining hauntings); but eventually every given vibrational frequency will seek out or be nudged to where it belongs. You fit your particular spot on the dial by your speed of vibration. You cannot coexist forever where you do not belong. Who can say how many spots are on the dial or how many frequencies there are to inhabit? No one knows. You shift frequencies in dying. You switch over to life on another wavelength. You are still a spot on the dial but you move up a notch or two. You don't cease to exist when you die. You shift your consciousness and speed of vibration. That's all death is...a shift.

Those who are not afraid of death may actually look forward to it. Such is the case of Carolyn Smith. She is a neat, very attractive, woman, about 80 years old, who has been a widow for a number of years. She was diagnosed with lung cancer recently and the doctor estimated she would have about 1-3 years to live. Carolyn had a great attitude about her coming demise so she started making her plans and preparing for her departure as if it was a trip to Disneyland. She cleaned out all her old stuff and decided to sell her home and build a house with her daughter - a house that would be a great place where her daughter could live after she was gone. Then her doctor told her about a wonderful new treatment that would take care of her lung cancer. She was actually disgusted to find out that she may continue to live! How dare they find a cure after she put forth so much effort getting ready to die? She said to her doctor, "So, am I going to die, or did I go to all this trouble for nothing?" Carolyn plans to have the treatment, but she is disappointed to have to wait a while longer for her ride home. Carolyn's attitude about dying is better than her attitude about living! Oh, that we all would have such an expectancy about our transition.

If you are dealing with fears and insecurities from old head programs, have compassion for yourself. Just love your insecurities, fears and resentments. Release and forgive them as they come up. Judging, beating or repressing insecurities just gives them power. Then you have a pattern that never gets resolved. Recognize that your real security is built from your relationship with your own heart.

— Sara Paddison, The Hidden Power of the Heart

Chapter Two: Fear of the Known

I must not fear. Fear is the mind-killer. Fear is the little-death that brings total obliteration. I will face my fear. I will permit it to pass over me and through me. And when it has gone past I will turn the inner eye to see its path. Where the fear has gone there will be nothing. Only I will remain."

— *Frank Herbert*

Maybe it's what we already know about dying that frightens us most; sorrow, confusion and difficulty. It causes us grief and emotional upset, a disruption of life, financial turmoil and a

14

total adjustment to not having our loved one with us. It is normal to feel that we can't go on or ever be happy again without them, but eventually our heart begins to heal, and we discover that there is more strength within us than we thought. The departed one, though, is not upset. Instead, he or she is an eternal, immortal soul who continues to live in a place more beautiful than we can imagine.

Perhaps another reason we fear dying is that we fear suffering—that of our own or someone else. A person's death affects us to some degree whether we are family, friends or professional caregivers. If you've ever attended the bedside of a terminally ill patient, you know that it is draining on the entire family. The process may force painful decisions, domestic challenges, or shifts in responsibilities. It may cause us to forfeit our social life or isolate from friends. We may experience any number of emotions after the loved one passes. We may feel anger toward God or another person, (as in the case of homicide), whom we feel caused the death. Our anger may be toward our loved one for dying. We may feel guilty that we did not show enough love or that we didn't do enough for them. We may blame ourselves for their death. We may even feel jealous that others still have their loved one and we do not. At times we may be in denial and expect, at any moment, to hear or see our loved one again. These are normal responses and part of the grieving process.

Critically ill patients may experience physical pain from their disease or injury, but they may also experience psychological pain as they become increasingly dependent and weak. They may be concerned about their children and how they will cope or how they will be cared for. They may worry about how the family will pay for medical and funeral expenses. They may also be dealing with their concerns about the life they have lived. They may experience guilt or a need for forgiveness in a relationship, or perhaps the need to reconcile with someone or say "thank you" or "good-bye". The dying process creates serious questions that cannot be avoided. Many who have gone through their lives unconcerned about spiritual issues may worry about what is to come in the Afterlife. Facing these questions may cause them to challenge beliefs they previously held. Without being physically or emotionally able to talk through such things, the patient may experience depression, anxiety, insecurity, helplessness and fear.

Family members may have similar concerns as they face the impending loss. They may feel that they have failed in some way. They may be reminded of a previous loss or they may be facing their own fear of dying. Due to cultural or religious beliefs, some families find it hard to talk about spiritual, personal or emotional issues. This only makes the process of letting go more difficult.

Family members are not the only ones who deal intimately with death. Medical staff and caretakers are also deeply affected by the death of a patient—perhaps not to the same degree as the family, but it certainly leaves its mark. Nurses who see a patient day after day form a bond with them and their family. A doctor may feel compelled to display a "stiff upper lip" and announce to the family that their loved one has passed. Regardless of how "in control" of their emotions they may seem, many healthcare givers are deeply affected by the loss of their patients. Dr. Aaron Milstone is the Medical Director of Vanderbilt University Medical Center's Lung Transplant Program. Due to the specialized nature of his practice, Dr. Milstone is predisposed to a high mortality rate in his patient population. He says that while the impact has lessened over years of practice, it still affects him personally to lose a patient. Routinely, people come to him for help once they have exhausted all other resources. They hope for a miracle from the Vanderbilt physician—a miracle that may have been possible had he seen the patient earlier in their illness. He says that the art of explaining death and dying, code status and post mortem requests to families is a critical part of medicine and patient care, but unfortunately it is also an area where many physicians are ill-equipped. He believes it is because so little time is spent in those areas during medical school or residency, and it is one of the great inadequacies of modern medical teaching. While he does not consider himself a religious person, Dr. Milstone does try to paint the picture of the Afterlife as a better place. He says that the end of life discussion needs to be generic and unbiased because one never knows the religious makeup or background of a family, and those beliefs may vary even from one family member to another:

> Each situation is unique and requires a very personal family discussion. You have to be tactful yet brutally honest and upfront, not withholding information from them. It makes no sense to delay or try other avenues. If you reach a point to where the discussion doesn't affect you emotionally or it sounds too rehearsed, you've probably gone too far and become too calloused.

When Dr. Milstone realizes that a patient is going to die, he says it is helpful to remind him or her and their family that physicians are only human, and that there is a limit to what medicine can do. Medicine is finite. Regardless of how skilled the provider or practitioner, it reaches a point where medical therapy may not be able to help someone survive. Some of the phrases Dr. Milstone uses in his end-of-life discussions with the family are: "We've reached the limit of what medicine can do for your husband, your child, your brother, your sister," and "Your loved one has reached the natural path of this illness and now we are going to let nature take its final course, and let your loved one die in peace." These words help families accept that the end is near, and then allow the staff to remove the ventilator or life support. When people understand that death is a natural result of a disease, there is no need for blaming anyone or feeling guilty about the decision to remove life support. A person can be kept alive for a long time on a ventilator or through mechanical feeding, but the deeper question is, "Is it what your loved one would want, and is there any quality of life for him or her?" Many times physicians as well as families carry out life support far too long. This only prolongs the inevitable and adds to the suffering. This is when a legal living will is helpful (see Appendix A). Having made a decision while in sound mind, allows a patient to stay in charge of their final days even when sedated or unconscious. It removes the burden of decision-making from another person and any guilt associated with those choices. Most families do NOT want to make end of life decisions for their loved one.

Isn't this a form of euthanasia? Yes, and this happens in medicine everyday. Everyone has their own opinion about euthanasia. Some people consider it to be a moral decision or religious belief, but I believe euthanasia is a form of medical treatment (see chapter eight of this book). Doctors are assisting in the natural course rather than trying to prolong the inevitable. The providers who are most opposed to "pulling the plug" are many times the ones who do not deal with death and dying on a regular basis. Because these are individual cases and real life experiences, there are times when Dr. Milstone will accommodate a family's wishes and continue unnecessary life support, but only for a short while.

"The mind is an incredible, powerful force over the body; more than we have realized," Dr. Milstone says. "It may be that the mind directs the release of certain chemicals like catecholamines that help drive the body. When the mind shuts down, the catecholamines stop being released and the body dies. There may be other humoral factors involved, but I am a complete believer that the mind is really what either keeps the body alive or lets the body die." Over and over again Dr. Milstone has seen a patient pass once the family tells them it's okay to go. He has seen repeated cases where a patient has, through false hope or denial, clung to life in order to get to certain events such as a wedding anniversary, a holiday, the marriage of a child or a trip somewhere. He has seen instances where the patient dies within hours of having been told the truth about the seriousness of their condition.

Commenting on near-death experience (NDE), Dr. Milstone said that his patients commonly tell him about seeing a light or going through a tunnel; however, just as common is their telling him about being out of their physical body and looking down upon a reviving or resuscitation effort during a code status. They explain an ethereal sense of hovering over their body and watching what is taking place. Once the resuscitative efforts are successful, they feel themselves being pulled back down into their physical body. Patients relay this to him frequently and he finds it very interesting and wonders why some people have the out-of-body experience (OBE) while others have the light or tunnel occurrence. Those who experience this phenomenon seem more peaceful and accepting of their impending death. When a patient relates this type of experience to family members, some are frightened by it, while others are comforted. Dr. Milstone finds it unique and wonders what that experience might be like for himself,

> It makes me think that perhaps there is a bridge out there to some afterlife. I don't know if it is a transient phenomenon or what happens after that period of time, but it is interesting.

Perhaps our stay on Earth is only a transition or passageway, and the before and afterlife is where we are more at home. Practitioners who assist patients in transitioning to the afterlife are facilitators or gatekeepers, helping us find our way back to God/Source. No matter what our religious background, we may find comfort in knowing that our life on Earth is not all there is—that there truly is more than meets the eye!

> " ... Men, believing in myths, will always fear something terrible, everlasting punishment as certain or probable ... Men base all these fears not on mature opinions, but on irrational fancies, so that they are more disturbed by fear of the unknown than by facing facts. Peace of mind lies in being delivered from all these fears."
>
> —Epicurus (Greeley)

There are many ways of coping with death. According to Elisabeth Kubler-Ross, a psychiatrist and prolific author of the ground-breaking book, *On Death and Dying,* there are five stages of the dying process: denial, anger, bargaining, depression, and acceptance. Every person eventually passes through these five stages. It is wise to allow yourself to experience these stages as they unfold and let others come to terms with their loss and grief in a way that best suits them.

Maybe you're afraid of what it feels like to die. During the research and writing of this book I talked with many people who have had a near-death or out-of-body experience. They confirm that dying does not cause a sense of loss, emotional upset or a sense of separation. During their experience they had no fear, sorrow or discomfort of any kind in the dimension outside the body. And where is this dimension? The Bible refers to this utopian place as Heaven. P.M.H. Atwater describes the dying process in two of her books, *Beyond the Light: The Mysteries and Revelations of Near-Death Experiences* and *We Live Forever: The Real Truth about Death*. She says that any pain to be suffered comes first. Instinctively you fight to live. Your physical body goes limp. Your heart stops. No more air flows in or out. You lose sight, feeling, and movement as if you are blacking out. The ability to hear goes last. There is no pain at the moment of death—only peaceful silence...calm...quiet. But the real you still exists. Your soul/spirit can still think, remember, see, hear, move, reason, wonder, feel, question, and tell jokes. You are still very much alive—more alive than at any time since you were born. You simply do not have a body to filter or amplify the various sensations you had before. You are not your body. It is just something you wear for a while. When you die, you lose your body. That's all there is to it. Nothing else is lost.

We've examined the known and unknown fears about the dying process, and the grief and loss we experience when a loved one passes. In the next chapter I'll take a wide turn onto a narrow, less traveled road and share true stories from people who have died and returned to tell about it.

Chapter Three: I Saw the Light (Near Death Experience)

We come to this planet with amnesia about our soul's identity and live behind a veil in order to function as a human being. The brain does not consciously remember where the soul came from, but it seems as though a part of the soul remains on the other side and is able to subconsciously participate in both worlds simultaneously; whether through dreams, meditation, hypnosis, inner guidance, or psychic abilities. There are accounts where the veil has been momentarily lifted or pierced and clear vision is seen of the Other Side.

People, who have clinically died and returned to their body, give remarkable accounts about life after death. The stories that many of them tell about the hereafter. are consistent with one another and may include:

- Someone to welcome the soul
- A guide to lead the way
- A review of the life the soul has lived
- A visit to a library or hall of records
- Periods of study or recreation
- A reporting to a council of wise elders
- An overwhelming sense of love and acceptance
- Other realms of the universe
- Heavenly gardens
- Sparkling cities
- Hellish surroundings

Many people are puzzled by these "beyond and back experiences" and are afraid to talk about them, even with their closest friends or relatives. Anita Ketchum Cooper shares her story:

I was nineteen and living in a cheap walk-up apartment I had rented with my 18-year-old girlfriend. We thought the place was a mansion. The two of us had just graduated from Business School and landed a job.

I invited my 12-year-old sister to spend the weekend with us. We were sitting around the table laughing and acting as silly as teenagers and a twelve-year-old can, when I got very tickled and the fish I was chewing got sucked down my windpipe. I tried to stay calm. I got up and walked around trying to get my breath. When I couldn't, I panicked and began running frantically around the apartment in a wild and crazy last claw for life. I knew beyond a shadow of a doubt I was going to die...and ...I did!

I traveled very swiftly down a black tunnel and toward a small round dot of light. I was totally unafraid to go to that light. The round circle got larger and larger and larger and just as I began to enter, a figure came between me and the light. I knew him! I knew him! I perceived that he was Jesus. He turned me back toward my body on earth.

Meanwhile my roommate was trying to call an ambulance and my baby sister had tackled me. She got me into a sitting position on the floor pressing my midriff hard onto my knees, forcing the fish to dislodge. I could finally get a breath. When I became aware of what was going on in the room, my roommate was still thumbing through the phone book to call someone. I told her I could breathe and to not call anyone. That night I cried and cried and cried and couldn't tell anyone what I was feeling. I could not go to work for a few days because my lungs, my sinuses, my nostrils, my muscles and everything else hurt so badly from my struggle to breathe.

The awesome experience of seeing something I could not explain or understand was more overwhelming than the fact that I almost choked to death. I had never heard anyone speak of any of these things so I kept it locked away in my heart like a precious secret. Thirty years later my sister and I were discussing the incident and I left out the part about going down a tunnel to the light and seeing Jesus. Then I asked her, "How did you know what to do? The Hymlick maneuver was not *even invented then and you did a rendition of that move."*

She replied, "A voice told me what to do."

That's when I told her the rest of my story. My sister became a nurse and I believe she was called to the occupation when, as a twelve-year-old, she saved my life. However, I floundered around until I finally found MY true calling—one that has taken me on a wonderful path to spirituality.

There are times when a person has an out-of-body or near-death experience and doesn't talk about it until later. October 21, 1976 was a beautiful fall day as my friend, my brother and I rode home from school together. We were hungry and after browsing the pantry for snacks, my brother decided to cook French fries while Kathy and I played duets on the piano. We settled down to munch out and were engrossed in the TV when we smelled smoke. I ran to the kitchen and noticed the electric eye of the range was still on high and the pan was smoking badly. I turned off the burner and without thinking I picked up the heavy pan to remove it from the heat. As I did, the grease ignited and flames whooshed up the cabinets and flashed toward me, singeing my hair and face. I panicked and lost all common sense. I foolishly picked up the skillet of flaming grease and started walking slowly across the kitchen toward the back door. My hand literally caught on fire, so I set the pan down to extinguish my skin. The table cloth caught fire so I picked up the skillet again and threw it through the screen door. As the pan left my hands, grease and flames scattered everywhere and I fell into a slippery puddle of what I thought would be my death. The tablecloth was on fire, Kathy's coat hanging on the back of the dining chair was engulfed in flames and I lay on the floor kicking helplessly trying to stand or crawl out of the circle of death.

I saw my life flash before me and even read my obituary in the *Atlanta Journal-Constitution*. My spirit was outside my body, even though I was aware of what was happening to me. It was like being in two places at once. Although I knew I had been burned, I felt no pain. Not knowing whether I would live, I was totally unafraid of dying. I was in total peace when Kathy pulled me out of the flames. As my spirit came back into my body, the pain hit me with a horrible jolt. I knew I was seriously burned. My brother was unable to reach our mother at work so he ran across the street to get a neighbor. The neighbor called the fire department, and rushed me to the emergency room in her car. The pain was so excruciating that I begged God to let me go back to that etheric state where I did not feel my body. All I could do was groan and suffer as the pain of third degree burns overwhelmed me.

After having a near-death experience (NDE), many people report that their fear of death is gone. That was certainly true for me after being so close to death during the fire. In fact, there have been numerous times since then when I have wanted to leave my body and go Home. That doesn't mean that I wouldn't react with panic if someone grabbed me in a dark parking lot and shoved a gun in my face. It means that when I think about dying, I have no worry about what is to come. If we really believe that what exists on the other side is peace, joy, a reuniting with loved ones, and the absence of distress of any kind, we would not fear death. Near-death experiences give us insight on the Afterlife. Those who have visited the "Other Side" have amazing and comforting stories about what they experienced.

In our modern age of medical technology many people, who would have died, have literally been brought back from the brink of death. Some have been revived even with no pulse or heartbeat. Some were pronounced dead for hours. People were discouraged from talking about such phenomenon and those who did were considered crazy or mentally ill. Some even ended up in institutions where they were given shock treatments. With the spiritual awakening that has occurred in our society in the past couple of decades, it seems to be more commonplace to talk about near-death experiences. The subject of NDEs has always been met with controversy, but they are not a new "trend" as some might suppose. Jackie Marten, a woman who is now 88 years old, shares an experience that occurred in 1952:

> When my youngest son was six I had a spell that nearly killed me. The doctor told my family that if I lived until morning I might have a chance to make it. He said that there were only two cases in Georgia of this condition and the other woman did not survive. During the night I had what I thought was a dream. The angels lifted me from my body and took me out of the house and laid me down in a sandy spot in my front yard. Two white doves came and stayed with me all night. They were talking to me in a language I couldn't understand. I could hear voices far away, and I saw a crowd of people wearing white robes who all looked the same. Without using words I asked the doves, "Where is my white robe?" One dove told me that I couldn't have mine yet. "You have to wait a while," he said, "You need to go back and finish raising your children." I was

disappointed. I didn't want to go back. I wanted to join the people with the white robes. I came back but I had no desire to be here and didn't want to live. It took a while for me to adjust to being here again. I knew there was a better place waiting for me on the other side. An experience like that never leaves you, and I have never been afraid of dying since then.

As with Jackie, many people who have near death experiences say that they did not want to come back. Many spoke telepathically with heavenly guides and understood that their journey on earth was not finished—that they had work left to do for the growth of their own soul and for other people. So they came back willingly, though often reluctantly. During a close brush with death people report seeing angels, former pets and deceased loved ones. Many times near-death experiencers return with their lifelong beliefs and their outlook on life radically changed.

Many children who are too young to know the difference between earth reality and other dimensions also report having out-of-body and near-death experiences. Many well-meaning parents who are afraid of the paranormal may discourage or even punish their children for speaking of such things. Some children who have had an NDE end up with IQs that exceed 180!

Medical science, which attempts to separate the physical body from its spiritual counterpart, tends to rationalize and invalidate these experiences. However, those who have had a near brush with death, come back with a better understanding or appreciation of life. The consistent message of NDE accounts is that God loves us unconditionally. Many report life-changing and long-lasting effects from their encounter with this unconditional love—some seem to exude or embody this love. Some NDEs are not pleasant or comforting. Some are downright frightening and negative. However, each person's brush with death is unique and includes what they were ready to see and hear. By coming back to us, they become great teachers who want to share what they have learned.

Researchers are finding that supernatural knowledge may be obtained through near-death experiences. Before his NDE in 1995 Mark Wray had little knowledge or background in physics or science; however, when he returned from the brink of death he possessed incredible knowledge about the law of octaves, plasma technology, the structure of harmonics, the table of elements, thermal technology, the string theory and other scientific/mathematical theories that are now being released and discussed by physicists and quantum mathematicians in scientific forums. During his encounter he was taken on a guided tour to the sixth dimension—the outer edge or threshold of the veil of creation. There he was shown how the acceleration of the frequency of tones becomes viewable as a color of light on a quantum octave level. If the frequency continues to accelerate beyond the cosmic ray, there exists a vibratory rate that is known as human thought. Mark's theory brings a new understanding of the New Testament book of Revelation. The book is not a prophecy of gloom and doom that many religions have made it out to be. The revelation has to do with quantum physics, the chakra system, the twelve steps in the chromatic scale and 144,000 tones or colors and the acceleration of consciousness in crystalline form.

During his NDE, Mark was given a choice. He could stay in the sixth dimension and continue his soul's evolution or he could come back to earth and help others with the knowledge he had obtained. No matter what his choice, he would be loved unconditionally. There would be no condemnation or judgment if he decided to stay. Mark did NOT want to return to the body, but he felt that the greatest good of humanity could be served if he did. He made his choice and is still looking for ways to share, explain and incorporate the supernatural knowledge he gained. The first seven years back were hell for Mark and changed him forever. The way he understood relationships after the event completely changed his family dynamics. His wife no longer recognized him as the man she had married. Mark wanted to move forward spiritually, but his wife wanted him to be the same person he was before the experience. This incompatibility resulted in divorce. Mark says that humans make things unnecessarily complicated. He is learning to keep life simple by not resisting the experiences that come his way, but rather to just go with the flow. He reminds himself constantly that he must be patient and allow individuals to each find their own path back to Source. You may reach Mark by mail at Mark Wray, 3007 Old Hickory Blvd., Old Hickory, TN 37138 or by phone at 1-800-428-6266.

Paula Forget reports an out of body experience she had when she was nineteen years old.

I was listening to music and drawing pictures when I began to see a grey tunnel to the left of me. I couldn't prevent myself from being drawn into the vortex. When I fought the current the ride became more bumpy and bouncy. When I surrendered it became smooth and I just glided. I came to rest in a place of total silence, peace and calm. There was nothing visible around me. It was a place of eternity where nothing ever changed, and I knew I would never have any physical needs there.

Since my soul/spirit was here in this place I wondered what had happened to my body while I was gone. Was I in a coma or what? (Maybe I was dead.) I was wondering what someone would find should they walk to the table where I had been sitting before I was swept up. I thought about my parents and wondered if they were going to be upset. I began to assess my life on Earth: what was the purpose of my life? I felt as though I could stay there indefinitely. I wanted to go back to my body but didn't know how. I had to make an effort to remember words because every thing I had been thinking while in this place was not "language" or words; it was some sort of telepathy. Finally I thought, "Don't I have to be somewhere sometime? Immediately I was back in my chair as if nothing out of the ordinary had happened. After that event, I have never been afraid of dying.

Many people have near-death and out-of-body experiences and don't recall the details of them, especially if sedated or heavily medicated. My second NDE was like that in 1988. I had been in terrible pain for about 14 hours when I finally agreed to go to the hospital late one Sunday afternoon. Upon examination and ultrasound the doctor on call found a large gallstone blocking my bile duct. Having no place to go, bile had begun to back up in my gallbladder to the point it was beginning to perforate. Even though laser surgery was available then, I was not a candidate because I would need an incision large enough to access and remove the stone from the duct without dumping the poisonous contents of the gallbladder into my abdomen. I was sedated that night and scheduled for surgery at six o'clock the next morning. My mother and husband were told to pray that the gallbladder didn't burst before surgery or I would possibly die from the toxins. I can't say why I wasn't rushed to surgery immediately other than a surgeon couldn't be located or inconvenienced at the time. I knew that this medical event was a possible exit point for me, and I was prepared to die. I was on pain medication and do not recall having a near-death experience; yet I know I had a significant spiritual encounter—either in a dream or during the surgery. When I awoke in the recovery room I saw a bright light overhead and was terribly confused. I asked a nurse if I was in heaven. "Not hardly!" she laughed. I moaned and went back to sleep. When I awoke again, the post-surgery pain hit me, and I knew I was still on earth and in my body. Boy, was I upset! I did not want to be on earth. I did not want to have to go though post-surgery pain. I KNEW I was supposed to have died and felt I had been cheated by being sent back to my body. I stayed angry during the entire six to eight week recovery period. I didn't want to be on Earth and felt that way for years afterward. I've read that it is normal for someone who has conscious knowledge of what it's like to be non-physical, to continue to long to go to the Other Side.

In my research for this book I was lead to Rev. Juliet Nightingale, a British minister and lifelong mystic who has been through a number of near-death and out-of-body experiences. By sharing her profound stories with the media she has generated a great interest and awareness of the phenomenon. Nightingale was the Membership Chair and is now the FOI International Relations Coordinator of the International Association for Near-Death Studies, (IANDS) and is the facilitator of Friends of IANDS (FOI) Nashville. Monthly discussion/support group meetings are open to anyone interested in learning more about the near-death experience (NDE), out-of-body experience (OBE), or spiritually transformative experience (STE). It is a loving environment where people can share these life-altering events. Here is Juliet's story:

> In the mid-70's, I was dealing with a terminal disease, colon cancer, and my life was ebbing away. I was bedridden for the most part, but could

sometimes manage to sit up for short periods. Being a contemplative person, I was always listening and observing—taking things in and trying to understand the deeper wisdom behind what was happening to me and where all of this was leading. As a result, I became more withdrawn and detached...as I observed everything round me starting to change. Solid matter became more translucent and fluid-like; colors became more vivid and vibrant; sound was more clear and acute. I could no longer comprehend anything printed on a page, because it no longer meant anything to me in my changed state of consciousness. It was like trying to read and understand a foreign language! I had already departed from the third-dimensional realm for the most part...and my awareness sensed other things.

I was entering into what I later came to refer to as the "twilight" stage. In this state, everything was altered. My consciousness was already making the transition from one realm to the other. I became more aware of other realities on other dimensions. I was seeing and perceiving things and other beings inter-dimensionally—even though I was still somewhat conscious on the physical plane. I've since realized that this is what a lot of dying people go through (such as those in hospitals, nursing homes or others in hospice care), while an observer might think that they're hallucinating or seeing someone or something that "isn't really there". In truth, they are experiencing other dimensions simultaneously while still on the physical plane, because, in reality, we are multidimensional beings.

I finally lapsed into a coma on Boxing Day, 26 December, and, ironically, declared "dead" on my birthday, 2 February! (Now I've got two natal charts!) While others observed that I was in a coma—which lasted over five weeks—I was having a completely different experience! One would look at my body and think that I was unconscious ...asleep...with no awareness of what was going on. Yet, I was very conscious and profoundly aware, because, in truth, we never really sleep; only our bodies do. We are always aware...and active...on one level of consciousness or another. Just the fact that we dream while asleep is an indication of our consciousness always being active. And, indeed, our bodies need to rest, so that we can tap into...and experience other aspects of our consciousness and being!

The best way I can describe the transition from being "alive" on the physical plane and the passage to the Other Side is like passing from one "room" to another. You do not cease to be or lose consciousness—your consciousness simply shifts from one vantage point to another. The experience changes...your outlook changes...your feelings change. And the feelings I experienced were profound. For me, it most certainly became that peace that surpasses all understanding.

My transition was gradual as a result of having a terminal disease—as opposed to a sudden one incurred from accidents, heart attacks, etc. I became aware of a "Being of Light" enveloping me. Everything was stunningly beautiful—so vibrant and luminous...and so full of life—yes, life!— in ways that one would never see or experience on the physical plane. I was totally and completely enveloped in *divine Love. It was unconditional love...in the truest sense of the word. I was in constant communion with this Light and always aware of its loving presence with me at all times. Consequently, there was no sense of fear whatsoever...and I was never alone. This was a special opportunity to experience being at one with the ALL— never separate...and never at a loss.*

The colors were so beautiful— watching the Light whirl all round me, pulsating and dancing...making whooshing sounds...and being ever so playful at times...then very serious at other times. Many things would take on a luminous glow—a sort of soft peach color. Everything was so vibrant—even when I saw into deep space! I was constantly in a state of awe. There were always beautiful beings round me as well. They were helping me, guiding me, reassuring me and pouring love into me. I was never alone.

One of the first things I remember was the life review, which included everything that I'd experienced in my physical incarnation up to that point. It was like being at the cinema watching a movie of my life where everything was happening simultaneously. I think most NDErs will agree that, the life review is one of the most difficult aspects of the NDE. Viewing your entire life before you, with every thought, word and action, can be most unsettling. Yet, no one passed judgment on me! I only felt the constant enveloping of Divine love from the Being of Light that was always with me. What I came to realize, then, is that we judge ourselves! There was no "he-god" sitting on some throne, passing judgment on me, (not that I expected to see such a being in the first place). I never subscribed to such religious myths anyway. I seemed to be the only one who was uncomfortable and most critical of myself. Yet, having stated that, I also realized that I wasn't coming from a vantage point of the "ego self" but, rather, from my soul self, which was much more detached and had no feelings of being emotionally charged. I was no longer identifying with the personality of the physical self. Therefore, what I felt was coming from a completely different perspective as the soul self—my True Identity.

Even though I was no longer in my physical body, I did have form—a body of sorts. The best way I can describe this is that I felt like a bubble floating and moving about effortlessly; sometimes very fast, sometimes gently drifting. I felt hollow inside and so clear—even having a sensation of a breeze blowing inside of me. There was never any sense of hunger, thirst, weariness or pain. Such things never entered my mind! Alas, I was pure consciousness, embodied in a light and ethereal form, traveling about or being still and observing intently—always in a state of awe. It was such a glorious sensation. I experienced such calm and a profound sense of peace and trust. I also experienced no blindness, (as I do with my physical eyes being legally blind), and what a sense of awe and wonder—to be able to see!

At one point, I perceived myself as being on a guided tour, visiting and observing different places, beings and situations; some very pleasant and some very painful. The best way I can describe this "tour" was like being in a circular enclosure of windows—each pane revealing something different.

When I'd focus on one particular pane, I'd suddenly see the pane become full size (much like a "window" on your computer monitor becoming full screen) and I stood still—just watching.

One pane revealed a scene that one might interpret as a "hell" or "purgatory" where faceless, grey colored entities moved about aimlessly and moaned. They were clearly suffering and in great agony. I saw these souls as damaged souls; ones who had committed unspeakable atrocities during their previous incarnations. I have used the analogy of a soul being "retrograde"—much in the way a planet will have the appearance of going backwards. The prevailing feeling that I had while observing these souls was one of deep compassion and a yearning to comfort them. I wanted so much to see them relieved of their horrible suffering. But, as painful as this scene was, I was reassured that these souls were there only temporarily and that they, too, would heal and move back in a forward direction and ultimately return to the Light. According to what was revealed to me all souls, without exception, eventually return to the Light

The above scene led to another scene where I saw images of people I knew in my present life; obviously those still incarnate on the physical plane, but I viewed them from the Other Side in a scene in the future. (Again, everything experienced on the Other Side is always in the "Now" even "past" and "future".) These were individuals who had also committed atrocities in one form or another— individuals who had severely violated me, or people I love. They were being made to suffer ... as a result of what they'd done—that, most likely being the karmic result of their decisions and actions. Again, I felt a deep sense of compassion for them and felt sad that they had to endure such suffering, yet realizing that it was also unavoidable. Never once did I feel any sense of anger or hostility towards these individuals. I only wanted to see them healed so that they, too, would come to know love.

Another scene I remember was that of finding myself observing a realm that constituted water. I beheld all its beauty and splendor and it was teaming with life. Then, before I knew it, I found myself under water and not having to worry about breathing! I was moving about effortlessly and mingling with everything that I'd first observed from without. The same thing happened to me when I moved through space...and danced and flowed with all the heavenly bodies and lights. There were lots of times for play and buzzing about with all the light beings—moving all round me like comets. This was an opportunity to experience great joy and feeling so light and completely void of worry or fear. I could move effortlessly...and adapt to any environment I happened to be in at any given moment. I would simply think about something and it would instantly manifest...or I'd think about a place and there I'd be! Oh, what a sensation to experience such power—to be anywhere I wanted to be and to create anything I wanted to...and to feel so totally free!

After experiencing the tour, adventures and times of play and creation, etc., things became more serious...and I was again in direct *communion with the Being of Light. I was now being asked to "help" or "assist" in some way...in creating and determining the outcome of certain events, situations or things affecting others! Me? Just little me? Oh my, I thought. That's a grave and serious responsibility. I felt so honored and so humble—being asked to participate in such a feat, but what if I failed to do my part as needed, I wondered. Then, I was assured that everything would work out exactly as it should—even if I couldn't complete things as desired. It seemed that the point in all this was the fact that we co-create with the Light and we are also part of the Light. Furthermore, no matter what happens, the Light Source will always be in control and be there to see things through, despite any shortcomings on our part as souls. How auspicious it is, then, to realize that, as souls, we are a part of all creation and take part in the actual creative process!*

This very thought of being asked to help—to co-create with the Light—made me feel profoundly special and important in the greater scheme of things, but by no means from an egotistical point of view. As stated above, I felt so deeply humble and felt a serious sense of responsibility for every thought and action I made. My only thought was that I wanted to do what was right. How important it was that I be very loving and creative and never damaging in any way … and that's the gift. I realized at that point, how totally connected I am with all life through all the universes. I felt one with the All—never separate, never apart. Still, there was no fear. There was only love. I knew I would never be alone. It's impossible to be alone, because life is everywhere—love is everywhere and this is what carried me and has stayed with me.

I so cherished this communion with the Light. Everything was communicated telepathically—whether with the Light or other beings, friends or loved ones. It didn't matter. It was always honest, open and real...and it was always done with love. There's no such thing as "putting on airs" and no need to hide on the Other Side. No one is there to hurt you in any way because there is no sense of lack or the need to "steal" someone else's power or *energy. You are operating as a soul, not centered in ego or personality. It's nice to realize that you will have whatever you need, because you've got the capacity and power to create it instantly!*

As the mood seemed to shift, I felt as if there was something serious that was about to happen. I was now being told that I was going to have to return to the alien (physical) world I'd left behind—that I was needed there for something very special and significant. I needed to go back to share what had just happened to me and to let others know that life is eternal and that death is an illusion. On a personal level, I was told that I needed to experience great love and joy in that world and then I would be able to return Home. I was then assured that I was real and that I could believe in what I'd come to know in this glorious realm—not only about myself but also about life. I was also told, however, that the world I was returning to was an illusion and that I wasn't to identify with it or be involved—to be in it but not of it—and that I was only passing through.

To say that my heart sank would be an understatement. This was the first time that I had the true experience of a broken heart while on the Other Side. The very thought of leaving this sacred realm where I was in constant communion with the Light and other beings crushed me in ways I could never describe. I knew how dark and foreboding that strange, illusory world that I was being asked to return to was. It is indeed a world I've never identified with! However, I was reassured that the Light and other loving beings would be with me at all times and to remember that I'd never be alone. Gratefully, there was still no sense of fear—only sorrow, but I realized that I had to honor the Divine will making this request of me.

As I reluctantly accepted this mission, I suddenly beheld before me, a most beautiful being—who appeared in front of me, pouring tremendous love into me and filling me to overflowing. This was my gift for accepting the painful request to leave my home on the Other Side and return to a world so alien to me. This being loved me very deeply and stayed with me, continuing to radiate love and sound. It was made clear that he'd be with me always.

I started moving back into this physical world in much the same way as I had left it. It was a very gradual transition. I was more aware of my body laying in hospital intensive care, hooked up to a life-support system, but it was still so separate from me and the vantage point I was experiencing from the Other Side. I felt like a newborn baby when I finally regained consciousness on this plane. Everything was so strange and new! I had just come from another world and this world appeared so much darker and void of color by comparison. Everything appeared drab and flat to me. I didn't feel the life-force I experienced on the Other Side, but I was resolved to honor the will of the Light I'd been sent back to fulfill. I had a mission...and there was a special promise that was made to me in return.

Even in hospital, I was aware of the Being of Light still with me and communicating with me. I was also still aware of other beings with me—beings I came to realize, later, whom only I could see and hear. Finally, one day, the Being of Light disappeared from view of my mortal awareness and I knew that I was fully back in this world. Again, I was broken-hearted, but still free of all fear—still believing and trusting in the promise that I'd never be alone … and so it was.

This near-death experience (I prefer to call it an Eternal Life Experience) left me feeling such a profound sense of triumph and awe. Something else I learned, too; is that fear is an acquired state, not a natural one. It is something that you learn, but it has no connection with the soul self. Love is the prevailing force at all times—no matter how things may appear in this world of duality and illusion. It's merely a hologram—created by the collective consciousness—for the sake of growth and evolution. Therefore, what occurred on the Other Side, for me, was a special opportunity to experience and know—with total certainty—that everything was evolving exactly the way it should, and that the ultimate destiny for every living being is to *return to the Source; The Light, Pure Love.*

The gifted, gentle and kind-hearted individual I saw during the above NDE was manifesting as his Soul Self and looked like wispy light formations—pulsating and radiating love and sound. The Soul Self is our True Identity or that part of us that is eternal and lives forever. Even though we incarnate into physical bodies, our Soul Self still maintains its form and is consistent and always the same. We have also got a soul identity [or name] that is likewise the same and never changes. Only our physical identities change—through various incarnations— as we evolve on our path that ultimately leads each and every one of us back to the Light.

Juliet's is a simply amazing story, and to me, more validation that we are only strangers on this planet and that there is a better place awaiting us in the Afterlife. Rev. Juliet Nightingale may be reached at by email at towardthelight@earthlink.net or you may visit her Web site at http://www.TowardtheLight.org. To learn more about the near-death research of P.M.H. Atwater, L.H.D. you may visit her Web site at www.pmhatwater.com.

Carved Stone

Your last words echo in my head
You held me close, all the while I bled
Now the whole world thinks of me as dead
Beneath this carved stone

It's lonely ly'n under here
Above, my name n' date appear
The words inscribed are so sincere
Marked on this carved stone

I'm restless lay'n here; the stifling silence fills my ears
Forgot the reason they placed me here
Under this carved stone

No children play'n, Nobody's sing'n
No one is pray'n, 'round this carved stone

—Gordon Randall Perry

Sorrow

In this sad world of ours,
sorrow comes to all,
and it often comes with bitter agony.
Perfect relief is not possible,
except with time.
You cannot now believe
that you will ever feel better.
But this is not true.
You are sure to be happy again.
Knowing this,
truly believing it,
will make you less miserable now.
I have had enough experience
to make this statement

— Abraham Lincoln

Chapter Four: Souls and Ceremonies

Three friends from Thibodeaux, Louisiana were asked, "When you're in the casket at your wake, and your friends and church members are mourning over you, what would you most like them to say?"

Gaston said: "I would like them to say I was a wonderful husband, a fine spiritual leader, and a great family man."

Guidry commented: "I would like them to say I was a wonderful teacher and servant of the Church who made a huge difference in people's lives."

Boudreaux said: "I'd like them to say, 'Look, he's movin'!"

- Unknown Source

Just as the birth of a baby deserves a celebration, so does the death of a loved one. It is a celebration of the life he or she lived, and it allows friends of the deceased to pay their last respects and offer condolences to the family. My husband has planned his own funeral. To save money he wants to be cremated in the backyard fire pit and his ashes used to fertilize our garden. He has asked me to throw a party in his honor. Everyone should bring their own six pack of beer or a bottle of tequila, some party favors and a lot of food that I can freeze so I won't have to cook for a while (Randy is the family chef, not me!) There will be dancing to 60's and 70's Rock-n-Roll classics, and our sons have been instructed to set off a huge display of fireworks in the cul-de-sac after dark. The media and the fire department will be notified in advance.

Most ceremonies are not as elaborate as the one Randy has planned, but I especially like the story Marsha Houser told about the celebration she attended in honor of her father-in-law's passing:

> *When my husband's father passed away, our family did not entertain grief or sorrow in a public setting. Instead we entertained guests and celebrated the life Rumsey had lived. As an alternative to a graveside service, we had dinner in the fellowship hall of the church where everyone told*

stories and shared memories of how much their lives had been blessed by knowing him. People were laughing, eating and enjoying the camaraderie in the midst of what some would consider a very sad event. So many times I've been to funerals and graveside services where I just didn't know what to say or how to comfort the grieving family. At Rumsey's service, we made sure everyone understood that this was a celebration of Rumsey's LIFE, not a time for grieving his death. It was the best party the family ever had!

As he had requested, Rumsey's body was cremated and his ashes were buried by a tree in the yard near a bench where his wife, Marlene, could sit and reflect when she missed him. To help our kids understand that Papa was still nearby, we told them that anytime they missed him they could go outside, look up at the sky, find the brightest star and know that he was near.

Let's talk for a minute about treatments available for the remains of a body. Some people believe that embalming or cremation is necessary or required by law, but neither is true. Embalming is done to preserve the body and make it cosmetically presentable for an open-casket viewing. If a body is being shipped via common carrier, it must be embalmed or placed into an acceptable container. Only a few states require embalming, and if cremation is chosen, embalming is not necessary. Embalming and mummification, (wrapping the washed corpse with cloth after application of oils and spices), began in Egypt and was the custom for religious and sanitation purposes. Egyptians believed that a soul could return to its body after a "circle of necessity" as long as the body remained in tact. The circle of necessity was a 3,000 year journey of the soul, after which it could re-inhabit the body and arise to live with the gods. Prior to the discovery of embalming, the Egyptians buried their dead in the Nile River. Ethiopians, Babylonians, Persians, Syrians, and Aboriginal inhabitants of the Canary Islands practiced mummification of their dead. Early Jewish and Islamic customs did not allow embalming or cremation because they saw it as mutilation or desecration of the body. Muslim practices today are similar to mummification, except the body is laid to rest in the ground without a coffin, generally with the deceased's head facing towards Mecca. There is no evidence that Early Christians practiced embalming. Embalming was used in the Dark Ages in Europe when great advances were being made in medicine and bodies were needed for scientific study and dissection purposes.

In the United States, Modern embalming started during the Civil War when President Lincoln directed the Quartermaster Corps to use embalming when returning bodies to their home towns for proper burial. Dr. Thomas Holmes, captain in the Army Medical Corps, embalmed over 4,000 soldiers and officers during the war. Realizing the commercial potential, Holmes resigned his commission and began offering embalming to the public for $100. However, the practice did not become common until the turn of the century. It was then that a person, who would undertake to manage all funeral details and provide funeral merchandise, became known as an "undertaker". Funeral services became a business that attracted representatives from embalming fluid companies. These representatives would travel the country selling embalming fluids (mostly formaldehyde) and teaching about the use of their product. Embalming gave ample time to arrange and prepare for the funeral and has therefore remained an acceptable and desirable method of post-mortem treatment in the United States and Canada. Embalming forms the foundation for funeral service business; but according to the U.S. Centers for Disease Control, it offers no public health benefit. Occupational Safety and Health Administration (OSHA) requires embalmers to wear a respirator and full-body covering while embalming; however, the release of contaminated blood and highly toxic chemicals used in the process are not regulated by any governmental agency and are commonly dumped into our sewer systems. Hawaii and Ontario forbid embalming if the person died of certain contagious diseases. Embalming is an expensive and physically invasive process in which special devices are implanted, and chemicals and dyes are used to give a restful appearance. While it prevents the body from returning to its natural elements quickly and naturally, it does not postpone decomposition indefinitely. Refrigeration will effectively maintain a body while awaiting a public funeral service or private home viewing by family members and close friends. While not all funeral homes have refrigeration facilities, most hospitals do. Many funeral directors will not allow public viewing of a body without embalming and cosmetic restoration because they consider seeing "a beautiful memory picture," as it's called in the trade, a necessary part of the grieving process. Yet, many people consider viewing a dead body a negative experience. According to the personal opinion of author, Elisabeth Kubler-Ross, in her book, *Questions and Answers on Death and Dying*, it may give the illusion that the deceased is only asleep which may actually prolong the stage of denial.

Other methods of post-mortem treatments include cremation, cryonics and donation of the body to medical science. According to Cremation Association of North America (CANA), cremation is becoming more widely practiced in the United States and Canada and is the post-mortem choice for 25 percent of all deaths. Cremation is a process of preparing human remains for memorialization in which the body is placed in a chamber and subjected to intense heat and flames. After approximately 2 to 2 1/2 hours at temperatures between 1,400 to 1,800 degrees Fahrenheit, all organic matter is consumed. The cremated remains, (also called cremains), are then processed into fine particles and placed in a container or urn purchased by the family. The cremains may then be retained by a family member, interred in a cemetery plot, or scattered on private property or at a public place that was significant to the deceased, providing local regulations allow it.

When I mention cryonic suspension services, (cryopreservation), you may think I've gone bonkers! Freezing human remains today in hopes of reviving the body in the future may seem far-fetched to us, but who would have thought a hundred years ago that the heart of one human could successfully be transplanted into another and give them a chance to live? Who would have believed, then, that a baby could be conceived in a laboratory test tube then placed in a human womb to develop and live a normal life? Did your ancestors read about cloning in their newspaper headlines? Cryonics is a post-mortem procedure in which a patient is prepared and cooled to a temperature where physical decay essentially stops. The temperature is maintained indefinitely in hopes that medical technology will advance and be able to awaken and restore patients to good health. I wonder if the same soul would return to that body or if a soul exchange would occur.

The last post-mortem option I want to mention is the Willed Body Program or what is better known as "donating your body to medical science". Studying the human body and its structure lends valuable information and insight to scientists and medical researchers in understanding and treating illnesses and finding cures for disease. Because the use of a body in anatomical studies requires preservation immediately after death, it is not possible to have a traditional funeral service. Many families have a memorial service without having the body present. Once the study is complete, the remains are cremated and either returned to a family member or placed in a memorial garden or interred in accordance with state law. A person must be at least eighteen years of age and competent to make such a bequest.

What method would I choose? I don't want to be gouged, drained or injected, so embalming is out of the question. I find an open-casket viewing very repulsive because I can't stand to be gawked at. I'm so cold-natured; I would hate to be refrigerated or frozen. I am missing so many parts due to past surgeries that I probably wouldn't be a good candidate for the willed body program. I love being warm so I suppose I would opt to be cremated in the backyard with Randy! For more information about eco-friendly funeral choices please visit http://www.funerals.org/faq/eco.htm.

Regardless of the method used to dispose of the remains, the passing of a loved one is a spiritual passing for those of us who witness it. The death of a close friend or relative has a way of opening our eyes and ears to the unseen realm. It also provides an opportunity for us to think about what we are doing with our lives and where we are on our spiritual path. We tend to contemplate who we are, why we are here and whether we are living life to its greatest potential. This contemplative evaluation can move us to create change for ourselves. For Jennifer Longmire the death of a close friend propelled her spiritual seeking, which in turn initiated a career change that led her to become a spiritual healer:

> *In 1996 my former husband, Bill, and I were living in Tucson, Arizona. We were good friends with John Payne and his wife, Sharon. Bill and John were in grad school together working on their Master of Fine Arts in creative writing. John and Sharon went through an ugly divorce and John was just returning to normal after grieving*

deeply. We probably saw John at least once a week and talked to him frequently. He was quite the character—big energy, deep voice—and he came from a blue-collar mid-western background. He loved to shock people and say what everyone else was afraid to verbalize. He didn't care what anyone thought of him and seemed rather gruff on the exterior but was really a big teddy bear. He was a gifted poet, and his writing spoke of the inner emotional world. That seemed odd coming out of this big, macho guy.

We had talked to John just before Halloween when he left to go rock climbing in the Dragoon Mountains at Cochise Stronghold. We got a phone call that he had fallen to his death, and when we learned that his body was being sent back to Illinois, we decided to have a memorial for him in Tucson. Our service was attended by John's Arizona friends and people from the creative writing program at the University of Arizona. In Mexico there is a Mexican tradition to honor deceased ancestors called Dia de los Muertos, or Day of the Dead. The Mexican Catholics have kept a lot of the pagan traditions; which I love. It was my visit to Mexico that sparked my interest in Paganism. I especially like the way they depict the Virgin de Guadalupe alone, not just as Jesus' mother, and standing on the crescent moon! Anyway, on the Day of the Dead, the Mexicans build an altar and place candles and photos of their deceased loved ones on it. Plates of food and wine are left out for the spirits of the dead to come and feast. The Pagans believe that the veil between the physical and spiritual planes are thinnest around Hallowmas or Halloween time. Dia de los Muertos is on Nov. 2nd. During that time, it is believed that we can communicate best with the Other Side.

In keeping with the Mexican tradition we made a huge Dia de los Muertos altar for John. We created an outdoor show of his poetry, which we mounted with photos and hung from trees. At the memorial, we allowed people to walk around and read the poems John had written. Then we came together to tell stories about him and share our feelings. We all spoke of how John lived and loved with wild abandon. Everything he did was with extreme passion and he died the same *way. Legend has it that the Native American, Cochise's body was never found and was believed to still be somewhere in the Dragoons. We imagined John and Cochise hanging out together. We thought we felt his presence in the room, and knew he was getting a kick out of the whole thing. To us it was so much better than a funeral or formal religious memorial.*

I had no idea how much John's sudden death would effect me on a spiritual level. I had just begun to explore my spiritual path. The following spring I quit my full time job as Program Coordinator for a human services organization. I had the opportunity to take some time off and really think about my life. John was a powerful teacher. Looking back, it was his death that ignited something inside me that sent me on a deeper search. It initiated a whole string of events that led me to my current path as a healer and spiritual seeker. From 1997-2000, I went through an intense period of spiritual growth that I think of as a shamanic death and rebirth. It is nice to remember John and the beginnings of my spiritual journey.

Almost everyone I interviewed for this book told me that they sensed the presence of their loved ones near them during the funeral, graveside ceremony and in the days following. In one of my lunchtime drives through the cemetery, I came upon a fresh grave and felt compelled to stop. As I sat there eating my lunch, I became aware of a presence in the back seat of my car so I started a conversation with what felt like a male energy. I nodded toward the mound of red dirt and asked him if that was where they put his body. He affirmed that it was. I asked him why he was still hanging around in the cemetery. He replied, "Where am I supposed to go?" I told him to go to the Light, but he said he was afraid to because he hadn't lived a very good life. I told him that God loves him no matter what kind of life he lived. Then, I asked the angels to come and assist him in finding his place in the Afterlife. I heard him thank me as he was whooshed upward through the roof on the passenger side of my car.

A friend of mine had a similar experience. Anita Cooper said that when she and her husband, Eldon, were going to the hospital for his cancer surgery, she saw someone approaching the side of their car. She thought it was a neighbor trying to catch them before they pulled out of the garage. She turned and saw the spirit of a man in her back seat. "We've got company," she said to her husband.

She began a conversation with the spirit, and he told her his name was John and that he was Eldon's brother. He said he wanted to be with him during his surgery if the "others" would let him stay. She thought it was strange that the man claimed to be Eldon's brother because Eldon was an only child and he didn't know who John was.

Much later, Anita asked Eldon's mother if she had another child. She said that she had lost a male child in a miscarriage and that his name was John. She had never conceived again, and Eldon never had children of his own. Therefore, John did not find a body in which to be near Eldon. Instead he was with him in spirit. Eldon then remembered the invisible playmate he had as a young boy and knew that it must have been John.

According to South African Shaman, Tommy Mueller, most souls attend their own funerals, and that spirit guides converse with one another at these events. He says to never go to the funeral of someone you don't like and pretend to be paying homage to them. The deceased spirit is very likely to be hanging out with the family during the "laying in state" and memorial services. Spirits can read the inner thoughts of every person regardless of the behavior they put on for the family. The deceased spirit is agitated and sometimes angered by the two-faced behavior of those they thought were their friends. Yes, spirits still have emotions!

71

Spirits waiting on the other side for the soul who just passed are also in attendance at funerals and ceremonies, and they rejoice that the soul has been freed from the limitations of the human body. They see life as simply a lesson learned and a contribution to humanity and the planet, but they do not mourn; only humans mourn. Contrary to popular opinion and the vision of the movie industry, spirits do not generally hang out in graveyards. They want to be around people, and funerals are an ideal gathering place for them. They are able to interact with human beings and may choose to visit their loved ones. This does not mean that they are anchored to the earth plane. Without a dense body they are free to be in more than one place at a time.

A dishonest visitor stole the ring off a corpse on the "showroom floor" (the funeral home). The daughter of the deceased was very upset and told a friend about it. The friend recommended a visit to Tommy Mueller. During the reading a spirit guide who had witnessed the crime gave an exact description of the thief—someone who had been in attendance the day the ring was stolen.

Mueller says that the personality of a soul continues in the afterlife. Otherwise you wouldn't be you! Jesus Christ appeared to his friends after his death and resurrection in a new type of spiritual body. Many people recognized him not only by his physical appearance but by his character and personality. They didn't recognize him until he broke the bread in the same manner as he did before his death. (Luke 24:28-31). Both before and after his death Jesus showed frustration that his disciples didn't believe the truths he had revealed to them. This seems to indicate that whatever beliefs a person holds in consciousness at the time of death will continue to exist until they are resolved and the soul moves on to another plane or mission. The "Tibetan Book of the Dead" describes an intermediate state called "bardo" which an individual enters after death. The Sanskrit word "bardo" refers to the 49-day period between death and rebirth during which a soul is adjusting or acclimating. This is the time that one is most likely to encounter deceased loved ones. That causes me to wonder whether there are stages to entering the Afterlife similar to the way a soul comes in gradually as a fetus developing in a mother's womb. Perhaps "bardo" is the "Valley of the Shadow of Death" mentioned in Psalms 23 of the Bible.

"For I am convinced that neither death, nor life, nor angels, nor principalities, nor things present, nor things to come, nor powers, nor height, nor depth, nor any other created thing, will be able to separate us from the love of God, which is in Christ."

—Romans 8:38-39

Some fundamental Christians believe that an "unsaved" soul will go to hell when the body dies. Since a person's consciousness and karma remains after death, hell could be considered the state of mind we create for ourselves while on earth. Mueller says that karma can be worked out in the Afterlife. I suppose that is why some people are concerned about a judgment of souls after death. In every NDE I've researched where the individual experienced any type of judgment, it was the higher consciousness of that person judging themselves. It was more of a life review to reveal areas that needed improvement. To me, this would be a helpful evaluation, not something to be dreaded or feared. In fact, it is somewhat common for us to assess our decisions and actions to determine whether they are helpful or harmful to our soul's development. For some people this is a daily exercise. For others, it is practiced at least once a year when they make New Year's resolutions.

Why do humans believe in a dark power such as the devil? When we make a mistake we might jokingly say, "The devil made me do it!" That may be a true statement considering that the word "devil" is referred to by the ancients as ego, free will or choice. The ancients did not personify or assign deity status to the terms "god" and "devil". They were symbols which represented choice or free will. Without the ability to choose, we have no power at all! Evil or devil is simply a shadow side of ourselves that we have been taught to hide because we consider certain behaviors or character traits unacceptable. The Bible teaches that there is no condemnation in Christ and that we should not judge, yet we spend a lot of time and energy trying to repress or get rid of something that is a vital part of us. Humans assign value to things, situations and one another by passing judgment or rendering an opinion. For example, our society believes it is wrong to be angry and that crying is a sign of weakness; yet psychologists have shown that repressing our emotions is dangerous and causes depression and other mental illness. We can find ways to express our frustration and allow our shadow side to have a voice without harming ourselves or others. I suppose it is harmless to conclude that the vastness of "God" or Divine Infinite Intelligence contains both light and dark. You certainly can't have shadows without light. Everything in the Universe is a manifestation of God in some way. Even the most negative energy is able to teach us a lesson. People like Adolph Hitler had purpose in life; they just operated totally out of their ego or dark side rather than from their spirit or light side. Sylvia Browne in her book, *Past Lives, Future Healing*, says there are dark entities or spirits who are estranged from God's unconditional love and are remorseless, manipulative, often charming and seductive. They are completely without conscious and attempt to draw people away from God by destroying their faith, self-respect, and peace of mind. They have no angel or spirit guide to direct them on their life's journey, and have no desire to progress spiritually. They do not go to a place of joy when they die; instead, they go to a hollow, bottomless void called the Left Door and return to earth in utero. They continue this cycle for centuries until a rescuer from the Other Side embraces them and brings them into God's light. Note that they do not have a "between" life time and therefore are not the ghosts or apparitions many people see.

Then, what are ghosts? Mueller says they are confused souls who did not resolve their emotions before death, or for some reason didn't fully cross over. This may happen when death occurs suddenly as in the case of a traumatic experience such as murder, suicide or a vehicle crash. Many times these souls do not realize that they are dead and will attempt to interact with their living loved ones. This reminded me of Patrick Swayze's character in the movie *Ghost* when he tried, as a spirit, to get his girlfriend's, (played by Demi Moore), attention. Personally, I have had my own ghost experience; like the time I put the scissors on the table, walked across the room to get something then walked back and the scissors were gone! I looked all over the house, and finally gave up on finding them. When I walked back to the table a little while later, I found them exactly where I left them. I thought I was crazy or going blind. Sooner or later these departed spirits will move on—probably to another incarnation where they progress at a higher vibration or level of awareness. It is not uncommon for ghosts to hang out in the auric field of a person who vibrates at a high level or has a lot of light emanating from them. They may influence a person's life in a negative way. Focused energy work or verbal command will remove the spirits and send them on their way. Remember the stories of how Jesus verbally cast demons out of people? These may have been confused souls who were looking for the light.

We've talked about spirits and ghosts, but I also want to mention spirit guides? We each have two or three guides to assist us on our journey. You may hear an internal voice, sometimes called intuition, giving you a mental nudge, instruction or advice. There are many levels of guides. Some are angels; some are the evolved souls of deceased loved ones. True spirit guides are of a much higher vibration than the confused souls mentioned before. They can be in more than one place at the same time. Their purpose is to teach, guide and even rescue humans when necessary. Some stay with you all your life. Others enter to assist on certain tasks or events then leave when finished.

Hopefully the material presented here will give you insight about interaction with your guides and departed loved ones, and help you appreciate those voices you've been hearing. See, you're NOT crazy after all!

An old man and woman were married for many years, even though they hated each other. When they had a confrontation the old woman would shout, "When I die, I will dig my way up and out of the grave and come back to haunt you for the rest of your life!"

Neighbors believed she practiced black magic because of the strange occurrences that took place in their neighborhood. She died of a heart attack when she was 68, and her husband had a closed casket at the wake. After the burial, he went straight to the local bar and began to party. His neighbors asked, "Aren't you afraid that she may indeed dig her way up and out of the grave and come back to haunt you for the rest of your life?"

The man put down his drink and said, "Let her dig. I had her buried upside down!"

Chapter Five: True Stories & Precious Memories

More than likely, each of us has a memory about the passing of a loved one. By sharing these inspiring stories we realize that after death our loved ones are still connected with us in spirit. We discover our own strength as we care for one another in difficult times. We learn more about our friends and families and bond with them in a way that perhaps couldn't be expressed before. Certainly, if you've ever been with someone as they passed, you know that the experience itself can change your life. It certainly did for Joanie Manogue:

My parents passed 45 days apart. Mom had emphysema and Dad had lung cancer. Mom never wanted to grow up, and since Dad was such a strong caretaker, she didn't have to. She enjoyed having someone wait on her. When we found out that Mom had only a year to live, we didn't tell Dad at first because we didn't want to upset him. I think it was a mistake not to be honest with him and allow him time to process with us. When he went in for a routine exam and the doctors found a spot on his lungs he became very concerned, not for himself so much as for Mom. He had taken care of her all her life and he knew that she couldn't make it on her own. We didn't know how much Dad had been doing for her until he started chemo and could no longer care for her. His two treatments were very hard on him. He told me that he didn't want to have any more and I said, "Then don't." I told him it was his choice and that he should decide what he wanted to do. I felt he needed to know that Mom didn't have all that much longer, so I told him. He was actually relieved to know that the burden of caring for her would not be passed on to the rest of us! Mom was in denial about her own illness as well as the condition Dad was in. Their 50th wedding anniversary was coming up and we knew that one or the other of them would not be around to celebrate it, so we offered them an early celebration. Soon afterward Dad was taken into hospice care where he went into a coma. He was in a coma and hadn't eaten in days. After a few days he rallied, sat up in bed, ate a meal and watched the Titans game with Mom by his side. He went back into a coma after the game, and we knew the end was near. We called Mom in so she could tell him goodbye. Ten minutes after mom told him goodbye, he departed peacefully. As I watched Dad's spirit leave his body I was not frightened. It was like watching him get out of a car. The body was just a vehicle he had been riding in. His spirit seemed to be hovering in the room as if he were checking to make sure we were all going to be okay.

Mom rallied for the funeral— entertaining friends and family she hadn't seen in years. It was endearing to hear people tell how much Dad had meant to them and share their stories and memories with us. After the burial

Mom went home, crawled into bed and started fading in and out of consciousness. Over the next 45 days, (when she was coherent), she told us how much she missed Dad and wanted to go to him. She frequently wanted to know which family members were in town and who else was in the house. Sometimes she conversed with her deceased mother as if she was in the room with her. One week prior to Mom's death, hospice staff began making visits to her home. The decision was made to remove all medical treatment. Her breathing became deep and normal even without her oxygen supply. A few days later her spirit left her body peacefully and without a struggle. When Mom left, she didn't hover or look back. She was on her way to find Dad.

The gifts of my parents' passing gave me were many. I no longer have a fear of death. I find that all other fear-based ideas no longer make sense to me. When my teenaged daughter was learning to drive, I didn't worry about her. I knew that she would be fine, no matter what happened. I've gotten to know my parents better since their death than when they were alive.

I am comforted in knowing that they are out of their limited bodies. I am now able to sit in silence with people and know them by feeling their energy rather than having to use words. I enjoy the comfort of silence.

Dad's spirit is with me still, and he lets me know it by bringing me the smell of cigarette smoke. I carry on daily conversations with him. I'll ask questions aloud and he will answer in my head. Mom, however, didn't visit for three years after her death, and then it was only after I mentioned to my husband that I wished I could reconcile the unfinished business left between us. The same year my daughter graduated from high school I began to dream of Mom. In one dream she told me to give the silver heart-shaped key ring to my daughter for her graduation. I didn't know what key ring she was talking about and it bothered me for days. I opened the closet and saw a box of Mom's things that I had not gone through. Out of curiosity, I took the box from the shelf and looked through it. I came across a small cardboard jeweler's box and inside it was a silver heart-shaped key ring exactly like the one Mom had shown *me in the dream. Needless to say, I wrapped the gift and gave it to my daughter for her graduation.*

Looking back, I don't know why we buried our parents in the ground. It seems so silly to have a gravesite to tend to. The loved one is not there waiting for us to come and talk with them. The body is like a vacant house—the occupant has moved out and the place is empty!

I am amazed at the love families are able to show one another during a crisis. My mother, grandmother and aunts cared diligently for my grandfather and my uncle during long-term illnesses. While it was never easy, it seemed that everyone inherited a special grace or strength to get them through it. Yet it is normal, not only for the critically ill patient, but also for those caring for them, to wish that the suffering would hurry up and end. Yet, as Tammy Roth discovered, there is a time to be born and a time to die:

About ten years ago, both my grandparents (aged 66 and 67 years) died of cancer only a few months apart. They were kept at home during their demise and we had hospice come in several times a week. Mom and I stayed around the clock, caring for them. Our family never talked about what was happening. We believed that both of them would get well. Papa's last moments were horrible as he gasped for breath. Everything inside him left and he looked hollow. The experience didn't change my view of death, but Grandma changed when Papa died. She had been a strong, independent woman who bossed him around, but once he died she began to glorify him. As she began to decline, no meds were given to try to restore her life. Instead we kept her comfortable until she passed on her own.

Grandma's body began shutting down but she continued to cling to life from March, (when she became bedridden), until June, (when she passed). She had no quality of life. She lost from 130 to 70 pounds. In her delirious state she talked to her mom on the Other Side and mentioned seeing the Light. Family members told her it was okay to go, but she still hung on to life for some reason. Getting "the call" was a relief. I felt guilty for wanting her to pass earlier. Mom and I went to a counselor who told us that those feelings are normal. I wondered why Grandma held on for so long. Then it occurred to me that if a soul's time of arrival on the Earth is planned according to the stars and planetary *alignment, then so must be a soul's departure.*

After Papa and Grandma passed, my mother became depressed. About eight years afterward, Mom opened to new spiritual concepts, started taking medication and began to pull out of it.

Whenever we have family gatherings, the photo of Papa and Grandma falls off the mantle. It's like they want us to know they are still here with us. I have dreams of Grandma; mostly about her being sick. It was such a horrible ordeal. Sometimes she gives me guidance and I sense her presence when I'm doing healing work. She was a hairdresser. I am now in a spiritual healing practice in a building that is shared by tenants who are hairdressers. Grandma likes hanging out here. In fact, today, before this interview, I drew an angel card that said, "Grace". That was Grandma's name. She wanted me to know she was aware that I was going to talk about her.

No matter how much we give or do for a critically ill loved one, it is common to feel that we have not done enough for them. Guilt can be debilitating and keep us stuck in the past. It is important for the caregiver and family members to heal their grief and let go of guilt. A dear friend of mine, Jake Matson, tells his story:

My grandmother had a stroke and was placed in a nursing home. I hated for her to be in a home and I was mad at my mom and Aunt Sue for putting her there. It was a long time before I would go to see her because I kept hoping she would get better. I guess I knew she was bad off and I didn't want to see her that way. Finally I met my parents at the nursing home and went inside to see her. At that time my grandmother was very coherent, but she looked like she had aged 15 years since the last time I had seen her. She couldn't do anything for herself and the home provided the constant care that she required.

On the 3-hour ride home I kept trying to think of ways to talk Mom into letting me take Maw-Maw into my home (even though deep down I knew it was a bigger job than I could take on). Maw-Maw did so much for me and I felt like she deserved better. I kept thinking how horrible it must be to live in a bed in a strange place with only a

TV for company. I vowed to visit her once a week.

The first time I went alone, I sat in the parking lot trying to talk myself into going inside. I hated seeing Maw-Maw in that condition. I walked in and she was so happy to see me. She complained about the food the home served, so I went to McDonald's and got her a kid's meal with a malt. She kept raving about how good the chicken nuggets and malt tasted. Since she only had the use of one hand, she couldn't eat like a normal person. It was very sad to watch her struggle to get the food to her face, only to have it fall out of her mouth. When it was time for me to go, she begged me to stay, "Please don't go, please stay longer!" she pleaded. I promised I would return the next week. On the way home I felt sad and vowed to go back the next week. I was mad at myself. I should have given her more of my time. Why did I wait until she was dying to spend time with her?

Over the next few months it got easier for me to see her. The visits were more upbeat. I went alone most of the time because I didn't want my kids to remember their great-grandmother this way. Maw-Maw was rebellious. She hated the food, she hated living there, and she fought with the nurses and aids. She asked me many times to get her out of there. She was more like a child wanting attention, and that didn't make it easy on me; I hated for her to be there too.

Mom and Aunt Sue hired a personal aid/babysitter. Why they hired a black lady to sit with an old New Orleans gal, I'll never know. It reminded me of the movie "Driving Miss Daisy". Every week Maw-Maw told me she was going to fire her. She treated her so badly, but Shea wouldn't stand for Maw-Maw's foolishness. She'd threaten to quit at least once a week. Shea must have really needed the money to stay with her. Truth is, Maw-Maw lived many more years because Shea saved her life more than once. Shea would stay seven or eight hours a day and Maw-Maw liked having her there, even though she would never tell her so. The aids at the home got used to Shea being there and they didn't do much for her after that. When I came to visit I would let Shea take a break. She deserved it! She was a saint!

Shea would have a wheelchair ready and I would push Maw-Maw up the hall and back, and sometimes I would take her outside. Maw-Maw lived for the day when someone came to visit her. Every week she would ask, "What did you bring me?" I brought flowers for her room every week, and we tried to decorate her room for every holiday. I always brought her something to eat and snacks for her to have later. I put up a bird feeder outside her window and she quickly came to expect that I would fill it during each visit. We laughed and told jokes. Once, I pushed her in a wheel chair down to a water fountain. I brought a fishing pole. We sat there and fished together and told fishing stories. I tried to make her laugh. If she was in pain I'd grab a nurse and ask if she could have a pain pill. If they told me she just had one, I would ask them to give her something else and let her think it was a pain pill. Maw-Maw would feel so much better then, not knowing she'd only had sugar water.

I would call my mom on my way to the nursing home and ask how Maw-Maw was doing. Mom would say, "Oh, she has good days and bad days, but the good days are less and less, and she is getting worse!" Mom even told me that I shouldn't visit her anymore. Still, I was full of hope and optimism—thinking she was going to get well and get out of there. After all, she had conquered every illness known to man. I thought she was Superwoman. She defeated cancer more than once in her last 15 years. She lost her hair twice from chemo and grew it back. She had pneumonia several times. She broke her hip and still went dancing around. She had cornea transplants twice in 20 years. Even after her stroke I'd bet she could still drive a car with one foot and one hand if someone would have strapped her in! In reality, though, she was dying, and most of the good days she had was when I was with her. Even though her bodily functions were deteriorating, her mind was as strong as ever.

As time passed, Maw-Maw learned to tolerate living in the home, but we always talked about her getting well and getting out of there. I usually arrived around lunch time and always brought her food. She was diabetic, and I always got fussed at by Mom and Aunt Sue for bringing her food she wasn't supposed to eat. In reality she didn't eat enough to send her sugar level soaring. She loved the vanilla malts but never finished a whole one. I would stuff her closet full of snacks and Coke and things she liked. No one else visited enough to know that all she took was a bite or two. I encouraged my sisters to visit and bring her something; ANYTHING to brighten her day. One day I was running behind schedule and was wondering what to bring. I figured I would be there just after dinner, so I stopped at a liquor store to get the fixings for a martini. When I arrived she said in an ugly tone of voice, "Where were you today?" She quickly changed her tone, "What did you bring me? What's in the bag?"— trying to grab the bag from me with her one good arm. I told her I was going to make Martini's. She said, "Oh, Jake. I don't know if I should drink alcohol with all the medication I'm on." I replied, "Just a little sip won't hurt." I set the bag of goodies to the side, having second thoughts. We talked for a minute or two and then she said, "Boy, are you going to fix us a drink or not?" I took a small Styrofoam coffee cup and made a Martini, poured half into another cup, then added an olive to each. She was so excited! She took a sip, spilling most of it on her clothes. She took another sip, spilling even more. Determined to get to the olive, she spilled even more. She couldn't have had much more than an ounce when all of a sudden she came to life with a sudden burst of energy and giddiness. She started telling dirty jokes, laughing and cutting up. She said, "Oh, Lord. If I pass now, I am going to smell like a drunk, and the nurses are going to think I been drinking all night. Don't tell Shea or Sue Ellen or we might get in trouble." I didn't have to say a thing, within an hour she had everyone in the nursing home laughing. Maw-Maw had her wheelchair comic sit-up debut!

Even though I was nervous about Mom's and Aunt Sue's reaction, I laughed for most of the 3 hour ride home. I called Dad to give him a heads up on what I had done. He laughed and thought it was great. I never heard from Mom or Aunt Sue, but a week or so later Shea wanted to know why we had a party without her. Everyone had heard about it. Time and time again, even at the funeral, many of our family and friends told me how she and the nursing home staff talked about that one visit.

In her final months Maw-Maw lost her volume. She still had presence of mind but she spoke very softly. She was not her feisty self anymore; not much on conversation. Every answer she gave was either "yes" or "no" without further reply. She slept a lot and didn't want to get out of bed. She seemed to have aged 10 years in only a few weeks. It was getting harder and harder for me to see her this way—an old lady confined to a bed. I skipped a week and didn't go to visit her. Before she would have fussed at me, but by this time she barely noticed. I skipped another week, maybe more. I couldn't make myself go to see her in that condition and I knew she didn't have much time left. More than once I prayed for God to let her go. I could see no reason why He would want her to live like that. There was no point.

The last time my two sisters visited Maw-Maw, she didn't open her eyes even once, but they felt like she knew they were there. My little sister thought it was time to pray. She took out Maw-Maw's favorite prayer, took her hands, and began to pray. Maw-Maw responded with tears from her closed eyes. Did she know these where her last days? Was she sad to be leaving or happy to be going? They all continued to pray through their tears. My sisters prayed well that day. Maw-Maw left us later that night.

I am glad I wasn't there when she died; yet sometimes I wish I had been. For a while after that I would get mad at myself. Why didn't I spend more time with her before she got sick? Why did I let all of those years slip away?

That must have been difficult for Jake, but what special memories he has of his dear grandmother. He was such a blessing to her. It is normal to feel the kind of push/pull Jake felt when someone you love is passing—especially if they have been a strong and independent person who is suddenly weakened by illness. I wanted to avoid going to see my grandfather while he was in the latter stages of his illness. My visits sparked him so much, and he loved having me there; so I kept going as much as I could. We lived next door to my grandparents so it was impossible not to visit them. My kids were five and eight at the time and they were not troubled by the change they saw in Pap, so I'd send them to visit him. They would crawl up in the bed with him and watch cartoons. It felt like a cop-out way of dealing with the situation, but I could only take so much of watching him die.

I'm sure a lot of people feel as though they didn't do enough physically and emotionally to care for their dying loved one, but guilt is not going to change anything. It will only steal your peace of mind. Since there really isn't a separation in spirit, it's never too late to make peace with your loved one or the situation that caused your guilt. If you feel like you have any unfinished business with someone who has passed, you could ask them to come to you in your dreams, or you can simply talk to them as if they were physically sitting across the room from you. I assure you they can hear you as you make amends or resolve your guilt. By doing so, you may release not only yourself, but your loved one to a greater degree of peace and rest.

Chapter Six: Hospice Stories

The concept of hospice began in England as a place where people could go to be comforted while dying from an illness. The origin of the word "hospice" in medieval times meant "way station for weary travelers". The word retains its original meaning when viewed from the standpoint that we are all sojourners on this planet. Today, hospices are state-regulated and only accept patients who have less than six months to live. It is a philosophy of care that may be provided in the patient's home or in a hospice facility. For many years people viewed death as a normal part of existence, and it was not uncommon for people to die at home. In fact, the whole process of caring for the loved one before, during and after death was something families did at home. It wasn't until the past 50 or so years that it became common for people to die in hospitals and hospices, and for funeral homes to provide after-death care for the body.

Our views of death may have changed, but one thing remains certain: we all need and want genuine, unconditional love. It touches and heals our soul, strengthens our spirit and enriches our lives. Birth and death, (entrance and exit from Earth), are two events where unconditional love is especially important. If you knew you only had a few weeks to live what conditions would you want around you? Would you prefer to be at home in familiar surroundings, or in a hospital or hospice center with access to medical professionals and trained volunteers to comfort you while you wait for your departure? Would you want your pastor or a member from your church to be with you as you make your exit? I would rather have a friend or family member with me, but perhaps you would prefer to die alone.

In an article from Dyingwell.org entitled Spiritual Care at the End of Life, statistics were given from a 1997 Gallup survey, Spiritual Beliefs and the Dying Process. The survey suggested that people who are dying want contact with someone they can share their fears and concerns with. Many wanted someone to touch them or hold their hand.

About half want someone to pray with them and help them find spiritual peace. Many who are dying want their spouse, children, immediate family members or close friends nearby. Even though many of the people surveyed considered themselves part of the religious community of faith, very few actually wanted a member of clergy to be with them in their last days. A person who is unable to control his bodily functions or feed himself is probably not going to find much comfort in the pastor or church member sent to "make the rounds to visit the sick and elderly".

Hospice care is not about fighting death or prolonging life with drugs, surgical procedures or technology. It's about making the patient as peaceful and comfortable as possible emotionally, mentally, spiritually and physically while preparing for transition. Hospice care supports the whole person—body, soul and spirit—and educates the family and loved ones about the process of illness and the final stages of death. There is a difference between cure and healing. Cure means that the disease no longer exists. Healing, however, can mean a healing of relationships, or self-worth issues. Hospice is not a place to find a cure, but there are many opportunities there to find healing, peace of mind, and enhanced self-esteem amidst isolation, loneliness, and other issues. Hospice gives the patient a chance to talk about the things that have been on their minds. Some people on their death bed discover that they did indeed have a meaningful life and a definite purpose for living.

Many people in nursing homes and hospice care are without the loving presence and spiritual support of friends or family. There is a great need for compassionate volunteers, but not everyone is up to the task of assisting people in their transition. It takes a special person to walk in, meet someone for the first time, talk intimately with them, and hold their hand, all the while knowing they may not be around the next time they come to visit. Yet, this blessed gift of friendship is crucial in helping a soul leave peacefully. Linda Woods (www.linda-woods.com) visited her friend, Irving Faust, while he was in hospice. As a result of her experience that day, she now volunteers regularly at a local hospice. Linda shares her story about assisting Irving Faust in his transition:

> *I was not prepared for the vision in front of me. Irving lay in his hospital bed unconscious, his breathing labored, struggling to let go. He was on oxygen and every breath was intense, difficult and uncertain. When I received Naomi's email about Irving's condition, I thought I would at least be able to talk to him, look into his eyes, and squeeze his hand. Not so. His angels had other plans for my visit. Plans that*

would definitely ease his transition, and plans that would shock me and change my life forever.

It was 11:20 a.m. when I walked into the room. His daughter Martha had flown in from Denver earlier that week and was scheduled to fly out at 2 p.m. that afternoon. We introduced ourselves and shared our memories, tears and emotions. I talked a lot about my relationship with her father, who had treated me like one of his own. He was always listening, always encouraging, always accepting. Now, here he was in the final hours of his life. After struggling with cancer for over three years and trying several holistic treatments, he had finally passed through the stages of death: fear, denial, anger, and finally and most difficult of all -- acceptance. I knew that Irving could still hear us. But how could anyone comfort him at this time? How could we possibly know what he was feeling? Was he frightened? Was he seeing into other realms? On some level, was he conscious and waiting for the moment when Naomi and Kathy would arrive?

I sat by his bed and the tears welled up again. The nurses were telling us that he would probably make his transition later that evening. I hadn't seen many people die. As a young girl, my grandmother had passed in front of me. I stood there helpless, with my mom, not knowing what to do. This time though, I knew I wanted to help, some how, some way. Intuitively I knew that I was a healer, but had never acknowledged myself as one. Being a healer did not mean that I could cure illness. That kind of healing only came from God. Being a healer to me meant that I could direct Source energy where it needed to go, and extend love, healing and comfort to someone in their most difficult moment. I had never actually offered my healing services. Instead, I was always promoting others as being more enlightened or gifted than myself. Oh, I had practiced my healing abilities on students in my Healing Touch class and on participants in my Reiki class, but never on a person who really needed my help, and certainly never with anyone who was facing his final moments. I knew about the power of intention. Anyone could use that gift to help others. And I knew about the power of "laying on of hands"— especially to comfort a young child in distress, or an elderly person facing loneliness, or anyone who needed the warmth and closeness of human touch. These were gifts that we all are able to give, with no special training, and I wanted to give those gifts now.

As I stood there, looking at Irving, a message raced through my head, "Do the 'chakra spread'." I had learned this gentle technique in Healing Touch Class four years before and had not used it since. It was designed specifically for people who were in transition and trying to make a decision, and it was certainly appropriate now. It involved working with the body's energy fields above seven specific areas, (called Chakras), including the solar plexus, throat, and heart. The message that I received was fast and fleeting, but it came on strong and I paid attention. I told Martha what I had heard and she listened intently. "I'll ask Mom," she said and picked up her cell phone. Martha was no stranger to Healing Touch. She had practiced as a Reiki master and massage therapist for years and knew the power and gentleness of the technique that I was suggesting.

"Make sure you want me to do this," I said, "because it's been known to speed up the process." Martha understood completely.

My mind began racing, "Who do you think you are? You walk in here during his final hours, and suggest something like that, when these people have been through so much. This is a family matter...and YOU are not family. How dare you come in here and suggest something like that. Another thought guided me higher and I knew that I had a genuine desire to help if I could. Naomi and Martha were more than receptive, and I could sense on some level, that Irving was receptive also.

When Naomi arrived, I could tell she was exhausted. She sat down and allowed me to help her relax with energy work while we waited for her other daughter to arrive. Kathy was on her way during her lunch hour, but running late. The moments ticked by. Finally, Martha said, "I think you need to work on Dad now."

I walked over to Irving's bed and spoke to him. "I know you are seeing angels, Irving. My angels are telling me to work with what's in front of me, and YOU are in front of me now."

I held his feet, very gently, and let the warmth of my hands soak into the fabric around his skin. At first, he seemed agitated but slowly his breathing became calmer. I remained at his feet for a while longer and then placed one of my hands on each of his knees. His breathing slowed to a steady, peaceful pace. After awhile, I raised my right hand above his body and smoothed out his energy field from his head to his feet. Opening his heart chakra was the next step, and I trusted that I could help him; trusted that I could do this, and let go of the worry, the anxiety, the thoughts of inadequacy, and the feelings of unworthiness. I just let go. I bent my fingers and placed the lower knuckles of each hand so that they faced each other. All eight fingers were pointed downward, with thumbs held straight up. I simply pulled my hands apart as I opened the energy field above his body. (My hands resembled a soft retractor pulling open the air above him). I did this motion several times slowly, deliberately, while sending an intention of love and healing. This helped Irving open his heart. He was barely breathing now. Naomi stood up and came over to us, placing one hand on his shoulder, and one hand on top of my hand, which was now stationary over his heart.

Then, in that brief, quiet moment, Irving took his last breath. All was still, but I was shaken to my core. Never did I think that Irving would pass so quickly. I thought he would make his transition later that evening—not now—not while I was working on him. Oh God! I felt so responsible for accelerating his death. Naomi, who was much calmer than I was, reassured me that it was all in Divine Order. I was meant to come to hospice on that day of all days. I was meant to be by his side to help him make a peaceful transition. The time was 12:10 pm, and Irving was on his way home.

I know now that Irving gave me the ultimate gesture of respect. He trusted me in his final moments and acknowledged me as the healer that I am. Irving's death was an experience I *will never forget and the catalyst that sent me on to begin my own healing practice. Now I am helping others in transition – no matter where they are in their lives, and I'm teaching them to be healers also, showing them how to use their hands to send love, intention and healing to others. Thank you Irving, for trusting me, in your greatest moment: going home - going back to Source.*

Assisting Irving in his transition was a very valuable gift to the entire family. It alleviated his suffering and allowed his soul to pass peacefully. The family had an understanding of what Irving wanted and were able to help him transcend.

It is not easy to address issues of death and dying with your family members, but the time of crisis is not the best time to discuss end of life procedures. It is a blessing to know in advance what your loved one wants and the only way to find out is to ask while they are able to tell you. It may be one of the best and most meaningful conversations you ever have. Plan a family meeting and make it a fun and intimate event. It would be an excellent time to sign your Advanced Directive or Living Will (see Appendix A). If you are unsure about what you want or if you need more information about available procedures please talk with a doctor or healthcare provider.

How can you tell if death is about to occur for a critically ill patient? According to About.com there are common signs that may indicate that death is actively approaching. These include:

❖ Major changes in respiratory health, buildup of fluid in the lungs, congestion, longer periods of apnea, and abnormal breathing patterns such as cycles of slow then fast breathing.

❖ Subject states that he or she is going to die soon.

❖ Difficulties swallowing liquids or the resistance of all food and drink.

❖ Marked changes in personality, acting wildly, severe agitation or hallucinations.

❖ Increased difficulty waking subject from sleeping, the inability to arouse them at all, or a coma-like state.

❖ Subject is unresponsive or cannot speak.

❖ Subject does not move for long periods of time.

❖ The extremities -- hands, feet, arms and legs -- feel very cold to touch. Subject may say that they are numb or cannot feel at all.

❖ Mottling of the arms, legs, hands and feet -- giving a blue or purple splotchy appearance to the skin.

❖ Decrease in urination with urine darkening in color or changing colors.

❖ Urinary or bowel incontinence.

❖ A continued drop in blood pressure to 20 to 30 points below normal range or a systolic pressure below 70 with a diastolic below 50 points.

❖ Loss of hearing, feeling, smell, taste or sight at the final stage.

It is important to provide a warm and relaxing atmosphere and be supportive during the time of transition. It is believed that the dying can sense people in the room and hear them speaking. Find comforting words to help alleviate fear or anxiety. Avoid crying or grieving while in the room with the dying person. Take turns with friends and family staying with the dying person so they do not have to be alone. Be assured that whatever happens is a normal part of the process and see yourself as being a blessing as you offer your time and love.

Chapter Seven: I Don't Like it Here! (Dealing with Suicide)

I suppose it is safe to say that most people have had suicidal thoughts at some time in their life. In fact, if you live in the United States you are more likely to kill yourself than you are to be killed by someone else. There were 1.7 times as many suicides as homicides nationwide in 2000. Those statistics do not include the suicide attempts that did not result in death.

In the October 21, 2004 issue of *The News Herald,* reporter Charlotte Parrish, wrote that more Tennesseans killed themselves last year (2003) than were victims of homicide, and that one-fourth of them were seniors. Parrish also said that teenagers and white males over age 65 have the highest suicide rate in the country. Why so many suicides? Experts say that suicide is usually the result of untreated clinical depression or mental illness. Stress on the job, social pressures, financial concerns, unresolved emotional issues, relationship woes, parenthood tension, midlife crisis, divorce, peer pressure, physical health problems, drug abuse and co-dependency are just some of the factors contributing to depression. A person may feel that their situation is overwhelming and that they have no power to change their lives. They may feel they have no purpose in life, or reason to live. With severe personal problems, suicide may seem like a reasonable solution to end or avoid emotional pain. It releases the soul from the body, but it also leaves confusion, guilt and grief for those left behind. A college student, Miranda Blankenship, shares the following story:

> *When I was fifteen I thought about suicide a lot. Even so, I still felt an intense sadness, confusion, and anger to think that I could actually go through with killing myself. I stopped wishing I was dead when I was sixteen. My cousin and best friend,*

Amber, called me one dreadful night to tell me that her father had hanged himself. Amber and her older brother, Bruce, had come home from school and found him hanging in the garage. That night changed me forever. I forgot about the selfishness of wanting to die. I realized how it affects people you love more than anything else. I don't think anyone who loves you could ever forget such a thing.

My friend, Jimmy, was silly and kind; a happy-go-lucky, sweet guy with a big grin on his face. He was generous and fun to be around. When I think of Jimmy I will always see his bright, smiling face and remember how Leonard Cohen's music made him cry. We were similar in many ways. We both agreed that people should always be dancing when a band was playing.

Once, I was trying to convince him to quit smoking cigarettes, he asked me, "Why should I quit?"

"You'll feel a lot better mentally and physically," I answered.

"I'll quit if you'll be my girlfriend," he said.

"You gotta quit for yourself," I said.

Jimmy quit for two days, which was a good start. It seemed to be the same with drinking. He told me he had stopped drinking for a year when he was married, but started again as soon as he divorced. He once told me that, underneath it all, he was really very shy. That surprised me. I always saw him as a very social person. He told me the reason he drank was because people liked him more when he was drunk. I feel the same way. It's so hard to know how to fit in and how to be accepted by others. Sometimes it feels impossible.

One night on the way home from seeing an all female band, Jimmy and I started talking about his mother. He told me how much he loved her and how he wished he could be a better person, and how she deserved a better son. He talked about how she had always been there for him and how much she meant to him. My friend told him there was still hope and that he could change. I could tell he wanted to change, but he had a difficult time with it. He seemed so sad. Jimmy was the kind of person who needed someone to motivate him.

I was leaving Jimmy's apartment one evening and forgot to give him a hug good-bye. Scott ran after me and said, "Jimmy will talk about it for a week if you don't give him a hug." I got out of the car, went back inside and hugged him. I'm so glad I did. I'm so glad I got to know him. If I hadn't pushed him away, he could have been one of my best friends.

Despite his caring nature, Jimmy was very troubled and had problems with drugs and alcohol. He was thirty, jobless, single, out of school, and living with his parents. One night his mother walked in to find him dead. He had hung himself. He had written on the wall, "Don't cry for me. It's selfish." My friend, Char, called me the day after Jimmy's funeral to tell me. I didn't believe her at first. All I could do was say "NO!"... I could hardly breathe. I was upset that Char hadn't told me earlier because I didn't get to go to the funeral. I felt like that would have given me some closure. She explained that she didn't know how things had been between Jimmy and me. What a dumb thing to say! Jimmy and I were not talking because I was with my boyfriend, Chad. I couldn't talk to

Jimmy because, when he was intoxicated, he'd say things that made me feel uncomfortable. I didn't know what else to do but pull away from him. Char was closest to Jimmy in his last months of life. They were together all the time and did meth (methamphetamine) together. Char wanted to quit, so she stopped talking to him. The night of his suicide he was desperate for a friend, but had no one to talk to. Jimmy's death affected Char horribly and she got worse with drugs. We don't even speak to one another. Jimmy's good friend, Scott, was like a brother to me and helped me get through the pain of losing my friend. I cried on the phone for hours, telling him how guilty I felt. I was so depressed to thin of Jimmy drunk and alone in his last minutes of life.

Jimmy's suicide was devastating to his family and friends. His mother will never recover from her loss. Jimmy took her heart with him when he died. I still have a hard time believing that it actually happened. I have mixed feelings about suicide. There is a part of me that understands the pain and hopelessness people go through.

There is no doubt in my mind that no matter what, suicide is never the right way out. Kurt Cobain and Janis Joplin lost hope for life. Jimmy Bagby and Amber's dad saw nothing to live for. Jimmy had a loving family and friends that cared about him. Morgan had a wife, three children, and a love for nature and art. Each had plenty to live for. It is from their hopelessness that I have learned to always remember the good in life. It is so important to never forget what you love about yourself, others, and the world around you. Look around; there is so much in this world to love. The world is so full of beauty, why shouldn't we all live to enjoy it?

Miranda is right. There is so much to live for, but when you are emotionally devastated it is hard to see clearly. I remember when I was suicidal. It began with several changes that occurred in rapid succession—changes that I had not anticipated or wanted. My kids were teenagers and I was approaching mid-life crisis. My daughter was hospitalized and then had surgery. My son graduated high school and left home. We had relocated so many times within a five-year period, I couldn't remember my address—four houses in three states. I had no local friends and the companions I'd left in other states rarely responded when I tried to reach out. The stress of these changes triggered an inner turmoil and I started having flashbacks of myself being abused as a child by my babysitter. I had blocked these memories so completely that I had no conscious recollection of the events. Once the memories started to surface with the domestic chaos I was experiencing, I had no tools or resources in place to deal with the emotional pain. I did not seek counseling because the man I was married to didn't believe I needed professional help or that we could afford it. He just didn't realize how serious my emotional condition was. There were many days when I didn't want to get out of bed, but I kept putting one foot in front of the other just to make it to work. At least my job took my mind off things; that is, until I lost my job. By then, I had serious doubts that God even existed and I questioned everything my religion had taught me. I had no one to talk with about my personal problems. The few people I did confide in judged me severely for not being emotionally stronger or for contemplating divorce. I kept my problems to myself until I literally had an emotional breakdown in my grandmother's bathroom on Thanksgiving Day. While I was sobbing my heart out to my mother, my grandmother entered the room and gave her advice, "Just hold your chin up and keep praying. Be strong and keep your faith in God. Don't let this get you down."

She had no idea what I was going through and her advice upset me so badly that I screamed, "WHY DON'T YOU GO BACK TO THE KITCHEN AND STICK YOUR HAND UP A TURKEY'S BUTT? DON'T YOU THINK I HAVE BEEN PRAYING AND TRYING TO BE STRONG?! I CAN'T HANDLE THIS ANYMORE! I JUST WANT TO <u>DIE</u>!"

When my mother heard the seriousness of my intent she insisted that my husband get help for me as soon as possible. A month later I was in counseling and taking anti-depressants, but I wasn't out of the woods. Twenty-one years of co-dependency, repressed feelings and legalistic religion were demanding to be dealt with. Even though I was making every attempt to get healthy, I still struggled daily with thoughts of suicide. I knew I needed to leave my marriage, but I was afraid I couldn't make it on my own, and I was afraid God would punish me if I tried. I thought the only way I could change my life was to end it. The only reason I didn't follow through with my suicide plan was because I just couldn't put my kids and parents through that kind of trauma just to find relief from my own pain.

One night in December, during an emotionally heated argument with my husband, (we had never before expressed anger toward one another), I fell to the floor unconscious. I was out of body and could not respond to my husband or my daughter as they attempted to rouse me. I could hear them speak, but I couldn't talk or will my body to move. I felt paralyzed. I knew that something spiritual was taking place. When I regained consciousness, I felt really strange. I didn't feel like I was the same person. I was physically drained and weak, but I had courage and a resolve that I didn't have before. That night, I slept in my son's old room, calm and in control of my emotions. I got up at six o'clock the next morning, packed my bags and walked out on a 21-year marriage. As I went through the divorce and attempted to get on my feet financially, I felt like I was walking through a fog. I felt disconnected to everyone and everything. I tried to pray, but found that I could no longer intercede with the fervor and intensity that I had before. I had a difficult time trying to form words and make sentences because I couldn't think straight. I thought it was just the stress and trauma of all I was going through. Maybe my nerves were shot, but why then, did I feel such a strength and deep knowing that everything was happening exactly as it was supposed to? I felt like I was being carried along by a current more powerful than my own strength. I just didn't feel like my old self and my own family seemed like strangers to me. I remember wondering if I had died and came back as someone else! What I didn't know until almost five years later, was that a new soul HAD walked into my body that night and took charge. This experience is called a "walk-in" or soul exchange. I had never heard of such a thing until I heard a lady sharing her walk-in experience. As she was talking, my body jerked and shuddered, and I felt a sense of knowing hit rock solid in my gut. The light bulb when on, and I knew that was what had happened to me. Later, I tried to talk myself out of believing something so weird, but I couldn't help but ponder the probability that I might be living as a walk-in soul. I certainly didn't mention it to anyone who could have me committed to a mental institution! It sounds strange, I know. I didn't understand the phenomenon at first either, but if you think about it, the concept makes sense. One soul is ready to leave a healthy adult body for whatever reason, and another soul is ready to enter the earth plane. The new soul may begin its spiritual growth and planetary mission immediately without having to go through the infant and childhood stages of development. Sometimes, and in my experience, the new soul is simply another part of the hologram of the original soul that vibrates at a higher frequency and has a more intense mission. The new soul will have to make adjustments to being in a body, and deal with the first soul's old issues, as well as heal its wounds and resolve its karma. That is no easy task, but it is still much better than wasting a body through suicide! Had this experience not made such a huge and sudden impact on me, I wouldn't have believed it was possible. Many aspects of my personality, interests, career and relationships changed drastically. For example, I was a musician who practiced as much as five hours a day before the episode. Afterward, I rarely touched the piano. Within one year I had completely changed my spiritual beliefs, divorced my first husband, married my present husband, started a new job that led me to begin my writing career. I have very few childhood memories, and the memories I do have are like watching myself on video or seeing myself in a photo, rather than as the one doing the action. These are common indications that a walk-in has occurred.

Back to the subject of suicide. While interviewing for this book, many people revealed that they no longer wanted to live. They said they felt like strangers or misfits on the planet. In spite of having a relatively good life and not wanting to cause other people to grieve for them, they just wanted to go Home. Here is a letter Angie Grett wrote when she wanted to attempt suicide. Perhaps it explains what so many people feel.

I realize there are many things I should have done differently and choices that should have been different in my life. The bottom line is that I feel I am at the end. Near the eve of my 39th birthday I am so very unhappy that I want my life to end. I don't expect anyone to understand because I don't understand. These should be some of the happiest and best times of my life. I have a fabulous job, a beautiful home, wonderful friends, and a loving 14-year relationship. What else could I possibly want or need? Peace—I desperately need peace. Unfortunately at this moment, I can't think of a time in my life when I felt peace. I can only remember chasing after the next thing, event, person that would make me happy. And here I am, 39 years of searching and pursuing. I'm tired and so very sad.

Many people will blame themselves for what I have done. Morgan, this is not your fault. You've always tried to make me happy. You were fighting a losing battle. I can't make myself happy, how can you possible do it for me? You and I shared the best years of my life. You helped me become a better person through your love and commitment. There is absolutely nothing you could have done differently. I say "I'm sorry" for the last time.

Mom and Dad, you both did an outstanding job of raising me with the knowledge that you had. I felt loved and special. You taught, by example, *how to work hard and strive to do a good job. Who would have thought I would get as far as I did. You were also accepting of who I was and never made me feel ashamed. I thank you for that.*

Jasmine, you are the best sister in the world. I'm so proud of you and what you have accomplished in your life. Don't give up on your dreams – just make sure they are YOUR dreams and not what you think will make other people happy. I feel my whole life has been about making others happy. My whole self-worth was wrapped up in trying to make people like me. Love yourself first, and people won't be able to help but love you. The things and money don't bring happiness; they just mask the misery a little more.

Precious, Emily and Jessica, I know you may not understand what happened or maybe you understand better than most people—you both are so wise for your years. You both are so very special. I hope that you both are able to know and understand yourselves well enough to know what you really want out of life. Be careful not to do what you think will make others happy. Pursue your dreams and don't let anyone define your dreams for you. I love you both so much!

I offer no judgment or condemnation to anyone contemplating suicide, or to those who have attempted or even accomplished such an act. However, if someone you love is talking about suicide, please take them seriously and encourage them to seek immediate professional help, (see Appendix B for signs that indicate someone may be suicidal). There are many caring professionals who are available to help. If you are contemplating suicide, explore the reasons why your soul desires to leave and what you can do to make changes and complete your mission rather than opting to commit suicide and destroy your body. If your mission is truly complete, then consider the possibility that you may have agreed upon a soul exchange before your incarnation. This type of exchange between souls is more common than you might think. Organizations such as "Walk-Ins for Evolution" assist walk-ins with their issues and support them in making the transition. Confer with your inner guidance and a talk with a qualified spiritual counselor who can help facilitate an easy transition. Either way, you'll still have to face your problems, but another soul moving in may have more clarity and be willing to make decisions toward greater wholeness. Based on this information, suicide is clearly not the best option because of the damage it does to those left behind.

Some Fundamentalists believe that suicide is an "unforgivable sin leading to damnation'" Others believe that those who commit suicide will come back as a severely handicapped person in another lifetime. Some believe it is an act of cowardice or weakness. It can be very difficult for a survivor to cope with their loss when suicide is shunned by society in this way. The loved ones that are left behind typically blame themselves, thinking that they were somehow responsible. Personally, I believe, when someone commits suicide, it's like dropping out of a class and having to start over next semester by repeating the life that was terminated. If we view suicide from the Abraham-Hicks perspective, we see that every death can be considered suicide because every death is self-imposed through the choices we make such as the foods we eat, the toxins we inhale, the risks we take, etc. We each choose, on some level, when we're ready to exit. We're committing suicide every day, some just slower than others.

Many people who have had a near-death (NDE) or out-of-body (OBE) experience either gain a strong will to live with a clear sense of purpose, or they become depressed about having to stay a while longer. Some have so much trouble adjusting to being back that they abuse substances or attempt suicide because they feel they no longer belong. Some think they are crazy (especially if their NDE or OBE was ridiculed or invalidated by someone who didn't understand the phenomenon). Clergy members, counseling professionals and medical practitioners need to be trained to understand NDEs and OBEs as legitimate, though mysterious, events supported by scripture and ancient texts. There definitely is more than meets the eye. We just need to train our spiritual eyes to see it.

To learn more, you may want to visit www.near-death.com where you'll find material on suicide, arguments about NDE/OBE, articles and stories about other people's experience, and a discussion/support forum you can join. For more information on walk-ins or soul exchanges see http://portaloflight.org/id35.htm. To learn about Abraham-Hicks, see www.abraham-hicks.com.

Migration

How do birds know when to fly south for winter?

Who tells them of the season's change?

How do souls know when it is time to cross over?

Or when it is time to enter the earth plane?

There is a voice within,

and angels about

that tell us when to go forth into the unknown

and return to Known

Midwives and doctors bring souls

through the womb's portal

but what a strong heart of love is required

to help a fellow man ease his exit

Rather than imposing your own wishes upon him

offer to open the door for him

If he refuses your help

be glad that he can do it on his own

—Yvonne Perry

Chapter Eight: Let Go of My Toe! (Euthanasia)

Twice in my life I have watched the health of a loved one deteriorate until their body could no longer support life on its own. It's like watching someone drown while holding a life preserver in your hand, except the victim has made a legal choice to refuse your help. In each case, a precarious but necessary decision was made—whether or not to allow euthanasia.

There are two types of euthanasia. Passive Euthanasia, which involves "not taking action" to prevent death, (when doctors refrain from using life support to prolong the life of a terminally ill patient) and active euthanasia, which requires an action on the part of a doctor or medical practitioner to "pull the plug" or administer a lethal injection to bring about the impending death of a critically ill patient.

Life support replaces a failing bodily function. When patients have treatable conditions, life support may be used temporarily while the condition is stabilized and the body is able to resume normal functioning. At times though, the body never regains its ability to function without life support. My grandfather refused to be placed on life support or be revived if he was code blue. My uncle, on the other hand, was placed on life support and suffered day after day while confined to a hospital bed for almost a year. Connected to tubes that fed him and machines that breathed for him, he could not talk or do anything for himself—things a healthy person would take for granted. Both my grandfather and my uncle were drowning. My grandfather refused the life preserver. My Uncle Edmond accepted a life raft with a slow leak in a sea of sharks.

Some people believe that it is not wise to circumvent the dying process. The late psychiatrist and famous author, Elisabeth Kubler-Ross, shared that her experience in working with thousands of dying patients and their families convinced her that euthanasia was wrong even for patients with terminal illness. She believed that euthanasia (which she called suicide) cheats people out of the opportunity to complete their unfinished business. The unfinished business she referred to is the contemplation of the ultimate meaning of one's life. She felt the "end of life" period is a time for resolving old disputes, mending relationships, and coming to a final recognition and appreciation of all the good things that have been a part of one's life. Personally, I believe we need to do this daily! Dr. Kubler-Ross believed that, despite their compassionate motives, those healthy bystanders who encourage or even assist in euthanasia are stealing the last precious moments of these patients' lives. I understand her theory, but I believe that every person's unfinished business must eventually come to an end. If one is unable to live without life support, and feels his business is complete, it would be cruel to force them or their family to suffer needlessly.

My grandfather was diagnosed with emphysema fifteen years before his struggle to breathe confined him to his climate-controlled bedroom. Much of the last year of his life was spent in a hospital. The non-stop care for his declining health was beginning to take its toll on my family who never left his side. My grandfather knew that he would not be able to recover from his illness and lead a normal life. Therefore, he signed a document in which he requested that he not be resuscitated or placed on life support in the event of cardiac or respiratory arrest. I remember talking with him in his final days. I asked him if he was ready to die. "I believe I am," he affirmed. He passed peacefully in the hospital without the assistance of life support.

My experience with a loved one's decision regarding life support, has led me to believe that every person has the right to choose. This is one of the reasons that compelled me to write this book. I believe a person, who is kept alive by machines against his/her will, becomes a victim of someone else's choice. No one should be denied the God-given power of free will.

USA Today has reported that, among older people with terminal illnesses who attempt suicide, the number suffering from depression reaches almost 90%. Even Jack Kevorkian, the notorious "suicide doctor," said at a court appearance that he considers anyone with a disease who is not depressed "abnormal." Kevorkian and others who argue in favor of physician-assisted suicide believe that even though depression is treatable; the disabling disease is not. Treating depression in critically ill patients will help to alleviate some of the emotional despair, but it does little to relieve physical symptoms. The patient will still lie on "death row" until the angels come. My personal opinion is that we have more compassion for our pets than we do for our dying family members. We will euthanize our sick and dying dog, but we will allow our loved one to suffer to the end. I'm not trying to pin guilt on anyone about any end of life decision they may have made for someone, I am simply making an observation in hopes of helping others avoid the end of life trauma that my uncle endured.

He underwent open-heart valve replacement surgery three times. During the third operation to replace his valves and repair an aneurism, his left lung was sliced open when his breastbone was being separated to access his chest cavity. The heart surgery was a complete success, which gave his family hope that he would make it. The damage done to the lung though was so severe that he was not expected to live. My family continued to hope for his survival. With narcotics, and the help of a mechanical ventilator, he remained unconscious for weeks. When he finally woke up, unable to talk, he was given a paper and pen with which to write. The only word he managed to weakly scribble was "DIE". Prior to this, he had signed a document which gave his wife, and his medical staff, permission to decide what procedures would be done for him. Because of this, he gave away his power to choose. Even though he expressed his desire for passive euthanasia, he had several more surgeries as his wife exercised the rights assigned to her in his living will. To my knowledge, none of his physicians conducted an end-of-life discuss with my family, (such as the type mentioned by Dr.

Milstone in chapter two), to help them make a decision about life support or to let him go and prepare for his death. Therefore, they continued hoping against all odds that he would recover. After several months of intravenous feeding, he weighed only 108 pounds. A tracheotomy was performed to relocate his breathing tube, in hopes of allowing him to take nourishment by mouth. He was unable to swallow, so another surgery was performed to place a feeding tube in his stomach. His body made several attempts to carry out the will of his soul, which was to die. He contracted staphylococcal infection, then pneumonia. An aneurysm appeared in the vein where the IV had been, and had to be surgically repaired. Then a drug allergy, an intestinal infection, Adult Respiratory Distress Syndrome (ARDS), and gall bladder inflammation threatened. The longer he lay confined to a hospital bed, the more depressed he became. His doctor prescribed Zoloft to alleviate his depression! My uncle wanted to leave his body, yet my family, with good intentions, continued to hold him back.

People with strong religious beliefs may not agree with my views on euthanasia. Many hold the opinion that voluntarily ending a human life is immoral and should not be legalized. The Nancy Cruzan case provides the U.S. legal framework for honoring the legal right of a patient in a persistent vegetative state (PVS). Nancy Cruzan had sustained severe injuries in an automobile accident, and had been in a PVS for five years when the Cruzan family petitioned for the removal of her feeding tube. Hospital employees refused, without court approval, to honor the request of her parents and co-petitioners, to terminate her artificial nutrition and hydration, since that would result in her death. The Missouri Trial Court ruled that Nancy Cruzan had the fundamental right to ask for the removal of her feeding tube. The court rejected the argument that her parents were entitled to terminate her medical treatment, concluding that no person can assume that choice for someone else in the absence of clear and convincing evidence of the patient's wishes. Nancy had expressed to a former housemate that she would not wish to continue living if she became sick or injured unless she could live at least halfway normally. The court, however, decided that the State Living Will statute strongly favored the preservation of life, and that Cruzan's statements to her housemate were unreliable for the purpose of determining her intent. In 1990, the US Supreme Court affirmed the state's right to determine its requirements for "clear and convincing evidence" and held that a patient in a PVS had the right to discontinue nutrition and hydration when sufficient evidence of their desire was available. In the end, a state trial court authorized the termination of Nancy Cruzan's feeding tube on June 25, 1990, and found that a person in Cruzan's condition had a fundamental right under the State and Federal Law to do so. In this case, it would have been ideal for Nancy to have had a living will which stated her end of life wishes in writing.

Back to my uncle. Before Christmas in 2001, after almost a year of struggle, my uncle's body completely shut down and he went into a coma. After five days his spirit came to me during meditation. He asked me to assist him with his transition so I began to sing, "Edmond crossed over to the other side today. Angels are with him, he is safe and at peace." I connected with the spirit of my aunt, my mother and my grandmother to let them know that Edmond wanted to leave and asked them to please let him go. I never spoke to them in person, but the next day my family allowed the machines to be unplugged and my uncle was finally free to go. During his visit, Edmond gave me the words he wanted me to speak at his graveside to comfort those he was preparing to leave behind. He also wanted me to play and sing at his funeral service and mentioned a few songs that he liked. On the day of his ceremony, I felt an enormous peace and joy even when the rest of my family was experiencing sorrow.

My husband, Randy Perry, has had a similar experience while working worked at Vanderbilt University Medical Center in Nashville as a Respiratory Therapist. The task of turning off the ventilator to allow a patient to naturally transition has occasionally fallen to him. Randy tells a story about helping a friend cross over:

I work with lung transplant patients almost everyday. However, for some reason I bonded with Jerry from the get go. I met him less than a week after his single lung transplant. I remember how anxious and apprehensive he was about the post-operative phase. He had a lot of questions. After his first bronchoscopy, I went to his room and started a conversation with him and his wife. I remember it to be a joyful experience, sharing not only medical knowledge but also information about ourselves and our families. After that encounter he was always glad to see me for his procedures. He would praise me and tell me he loved me and how thankful he was. His lung transplant was a blessing to him because it allowed him to have his wish to live long enough to see his daughter get married.

From the time of his transplant to the time of his passing, Jerry had one complication after another, but his strong Spirit never waned. After eight months his new lung stopped functioning and his native lung was in horrible condition. He was placed on a ventilator with the hope that it might give him time to recover, but it was not meant to be. Jerry had not wanted to be placed on the ventilator. After three days, his doctor asked me to talk with the family because he knew how close we were. His beautiful, loving family and friends gathered to give Jerry their love and to say their farewells. It is believed that your hearing is the last of the five senses to dissipate, and even though Jerry was well-sedated, I'm sure he could hear them when they told him how much he had blessed their lives, (he had led many to know of Jesus). The ventilator was turned off and removed but he did not pass immediately. In fact, his blood oxygen level actually improved as his friends and family ministered to him. As they sang hymns in his room that afternoon, I could see a pink and purple aura around his face and head. There were some who did not want Jerry to go and they were essentially grounding him by holding onto his feet and hands. This went on for many hours. Before I left for the day I told Jerry how much he meant to me. It was not until after *midnight that his spirit departed. I believe Jerry's life mission was fulfilled and he left us at an early age because he has another mission to accomplish. I have no doubt he will be as successful in the next life as he was in this one. I am so grateful for the privilege of having known such a loving human being.*

It's never easy to let someone go, but it can be a peaceful experience when we realize the favor we are doing them by setting them free.

Sister Sarah was getting old. One day after church services the minister came to her and said, "Sister, you are getting along in years and I was wondering if you have given any thought to the hereafter."

"Why, Reverend," she replied, "I think about the hereafter all the time. I walk from the living room to the kitchen and think to myself 'What did I come in here after?'"

—Unknown Source

Chapter Nine: Knock, Knock. Who's There? (Spirit Visits)

Why do some people see, hear or sense the presence of departed loved ones, angels or spirit guides while others do not? Possibly some people are more psychic than others because they have been equipped or gifted with these tools in order to fulfill their life's mission. Maybe they are here to serve as intuitive healers, psychic detectives, spiritual readers—occupations that require the ability to converse with the other side. I believe that everyone has some degree of psychic ability that can be developed. Maybe you hear and see in the spirit world, but don't acknowledge it or want to admit it! In Jesus said over and over again, "Blessed are those who have eyes to see and ears to hear." Perhaps he was referring to those who can see through the veil that separates the world of physical and non-physical. Some say that seeing is believing, but I think that one must believe before they can see. Everything that we call "reality" exists because we believed, at some point, that it could be. Whether it's drawing a picture, rearranging your furniture, decorating a cake, making a golf shot or inventing a new tool; whenever you create something, you at least have a mental concept of what it might look like or how it might operate. The Bible says that God calls those things that are not, as if they already are. In other words, what you believe affects what you experience. The good news is you can always change what you believe! Following are some ways to enhance your ability to see and hear in other dimensions and to interact with angels and deceased loved ones:

- ❖ Practice thoughts of non-separation (believe you can see/hear)

- ❖ Remove limiting beliefs and self-talk

- ❖ Heal past wounds that block the psychic gateways

❖ Practice energy work (such as Reiki) to remove clutter from your auric field or space

❖ Train your eye to see finer vibrations (learn to read auras). Also watch for plasma splotches or multi-colored sparkling light trails when in a dark or dimly lit room. You may get mental pictures rather than seeing with your physical eyes.

❖ Listen quietly during meditation. The most common way people experience the Other Side is through an internal voice that may sound like their own voice or the voice of their loved one.

❖ Be aware of an energy shift around you or a change in temperature in the environment. This may feel similar to the times when you've caught someone staring at you from across the room—you could "feel" them looking at you.

❖ Trust any sense of "knowing" you get. We all have intuition!

I realize that many people are afraid they might contact the wrong person or be possessed by an evil spirit or get into trouble with dark entities. When I was doing spiritual warfare, (as taught by the church I was attending) I encountered all kinds of entities and my energy field was being infiltrated by lost souls looking for their way Home. I didn't know what was happening, but I was hearing some awful things in my head. Now, I know how to help souls cross over and protect myself from being vulnerable. Dark beings gravitate to fear, but they are repelled by love and light. Simply send a mental beam of love and light to the dark entity and it will flee. When I stopped giving power to the belief (or expectation) that I would contact dark entities, they automatically stopped showing up. I can still feel negative energy in or around a person, but I remind myself that we are all one in God and that nothing can harm me unless I open myself to allow it. Remember that we are never working alone; we have helpers of the Highest Light to assist us. If you have closed your psychic powers down because you are afraid, simply ask the angels to put a hedge around you and protect you from all harm or evil, and allow you to connect only with the light beings who are willing and able to assist you in doing God's will. As you begin to trust your guidance and intuition, you will find that you receive only God's highest and best. Then you will be able to assist souls on both sides of the veil without fear.

After my grandfather, Pap, passed away in 1988, his energy and spirit continued to be with our family. My grandmother reported many occasions when she saw him in her bedroom at night, talked to him throughout her day, or conversed with him in her dreams. My brother's son was not yet born when Pap passed, but when he was three years old he began to tell his mom that Pap was in his room at night and that he was afraid of him. Knowing my grandfather as the prankster and practical joker that he was, he may have been teasing the toddler. My brother's wife did not like the idea of a ghost in her son's room so she asked Pap to leave and to never come back. He has not visited them since. My daughter-in-law has also mentioned having visits from Pap even though she didn't know him while he was alive. After ten years, all family members stopped receiving visits from him. I wondered why, but I assumed he had a good reason for moving on.

About a week after my uncle passed, I heard him speaking to me in my head. He told me he had connected with his father. "Pap is in school", he said. I laughed at the prospect of my grandfather being a student. I imagined him wearing a dunce cap or having "time out" for acting as class clown or picking on the girls! "Why is he in school?" I asked. "He's learning his lessons!" he replied. We both laughed. My uncle explained, "It's not a typical school like you have on Earth. Pap is in a "review and redo" conference with his guides and angels to negotiate his next life's contract." In other words, he was preparing to reincarnate.

Our deceased loved ones want us to know that they are okay and that they are still concerned for our welfare. One woman told me she had a visit the night of her mother's funeral. Her mother had been ill for a long time and suffered greatly before she passed. The woman was sitting in her bedroom when she audibly heard the voice of her mother say, "I just wanted to let you know I'm fine now." It seems that many deceased loved ones continue to linger around their family. I'm not sure why some choose to make their presence known while others do not, but perhaps Vickie Majors' story will shed some light.

My father died in 1990. We were so close that I just knew he would come to me. Many years passed and I gave up on the idea of hearing from him. When I was going through my divorce in 2000, he finally came to visit. I was in a deep depression. Most of my inspiration comes to me when I sleep or when I am slightly awake in the early hours of the morning, and that was when I heard my father's voice. He was at the foot of my bed and looked just like he did before he got sick. He appeared to be in the form of a mirage or a hologram. I asked him why he hadn't visited me earlier. He said that I hadn't needed him before. He wanted me to know that he was fine and that I was going to be fine too. He said he was always close by, watching over Mama and me. He said he was proud of me and that he loved me.

His visit brought me tremendous peace during that very difficult time in my life. I've known of his presence since then and have heard his voice, but have never seen his image again. And now, as I write this I can still feel his presence. Sometimes I experience a tingling down the whole right side of my body. It grows stronger, and at times it will immobilize me and my hair stands on end. I remain still while the sensation subsides, then I speak to my dad and acknowledge his presence. I also try to listen to what he is trying to tell me. I feel so incredibly loved and blessed after one of these episodes. It doesn't happen very often but I wish it would. I LOVE to feel his presence.

Vickie's story is comforting. It reminds me of the kind and nurturing being who stayed near me on those lonely nights when I was processing through my divorce. It seemed that whenever I cried, this loving presence touched me in a warm and motherly way. I assumed it was an angel so I began to ask for her to touch me. She always complied, and I could feel her soothing warmth envelope me as she caressed my shoulders and back. When I met my current husband, Randy, my life became full of love. With his arms around me and didn't really notice when the presence stopped visiting me.

One day during meditation, I asked my spirit guide to introduce me to some of the other beings who assist me on my journey. There was Ginny Lee, the mothering spirit who had consoled me during my divorce. He said that she had lived in the U.S. within the past decade, and had passed only a few years ago. He said she was a mother with a great sense of humor, who loved to care for people, and that she was the one who led me to the church where I met Randy. I was so overwhelmed by this revelation that I started crying, and when I did, I felt those sweet, tender arms around me just like before! I shared my story with Randy and his mouth fell open, "You have just described my mother to a tee," he said. "Her name was Virginia Lee, but people who were close to her called her Ginny Lee! She kept everyone laughing until she died suddenly three years ago." That was about the same time I started sensing her presence. Randy and I realized that his mom had chosen to leave her physical body in order to complete a Divine assignment—to bring the two of us together. We set a plate for her at the dinner table that night to honor her and thank her for blessing our lives. I rejoice now, knowing that those who pass to the other side still have missions and want to assist us in our earthly journey.

Sometimes, deceased loved ones stop by for a visit, just to check in with us or show us that they are alive in a different form. After his death, Jesus manifested in a modified human form and was able to appear and disappear at will. He ate and drank food and was able to disguise himself so that others didn't recognize him even though he retained his physical characteristics (Luke 24:36-39). A similar thing occurred when Randy and I drove to visit my family in Georgia after my uncle Edmond died. We stopped at a convenience store to pump gas and I stayed in the car while Randy went inside to pay. A man walked out of the store that looked just like my uncle when he was 40 years old and in good health. He was wearing jeans and an unzipped blue denim jacket that had a red and black plaid lining. Edmond was a smoker and he loved Jack Daniels and Coke. My mouth fell open as I watched this man try to open a pack of cigarettes with one hand and hold a Coke with the other. He had a little brown sack under his arm about the size and shape of a pint of whiskey. He sat the Coke down on the trash can, lit a cigarette and looked right at me. He seemed to know me and I was paralyzed, unable to move or speak. His physical features and mannerisms were identical to my uncle. Then he walked by the driver's side of our car. My heart was pounding and I tried not to stare. As he neared the back door I turned to get another look at him, but he had vanished. I turned completely around in my seat and scanned the parking lot in all directions, but there was no trace of him.

Randy returned to the car. "Did you see him?" I asked excitedly.

"Who?"

"My uncle, Edmond! That man who came out of the store with the Coke and cigarettes?" "He was my uncle's spirit! I KNOW I saw him!"

I was ecstatic! Randy just looked at me, not really knowing what to say

"Well, he was here!" I announced. "I just saw him."

Our non-physical loved ones don't always appear in human form when they come to let us know they are okay. Sometimes they appear in disguise. Lisa Moran tells her story:

> *In the summer of 1991 I went on vacation at a macrobiotic health resort in Estes Park, Colorado. My one week vacation turned into two weeks, and then a sabbatical from work for a couple of months. I paid my way at the resort by keeping the books. By the end of the summer, I felt led to move to Colorado.*

My consulting job was 100% travel, but my employer didn't accept my proposal to work from the Denver airport. So I quit. Over the next year, I became a certified Pilates instructor, opened a studio and began teaching Pilates strength and flexibility techniques to dancers and other residents in the Fort Collins area.

Randy was the choreographer for the local dance company. He had a tall, thin frame with dark hair and he had a distinct way of making ballet fun and playful. Randy participated in several Pilates mat classes at our studio and helped promote our business among the dancers. When I attended a performance of the ballet company, I was very impressed with Randy's choreography. As I became more integrated in the community I served on the Board of Directors and then became the Board President for the ballet. Randy and I worked together on several projects.

Colorado was far too cold for my liking and after a few years I moved to Phoenix, Arizona to warm up. I was saddened to learn that Randy had AIDS and was becoming ill. The ballet needed someone to train with Randy while he still had the ability to dance and mentor. The company received an application from a dancer/instructor in Phoenix, and called me to do a first interview. Oddly enough, the job candidate was named 'Byrd'. After passing my interview (I thought Byrd was delightful!) he was interviewed and hired by the ballet. Byrd moved to Fort Collins and started the job, but it was only a few weeks after his arrival when Randy died.

Byrd called me at 6 a.m. the next morning to tell me Randy passed on. As I left my house a few minutes later and drove slowly toward the stop sign at the end of my street, a dove swooped over the top of my car, down the windshield and across the hood, swaying from side to side with wings outstretched. He landed a few feet in front of my car and strutted to the side of the road. He then turned around and stared at me. I knew it was Randy telling me he was fine. Randy dancing in the after life.

I've heard from the Abraham-Hicks teaching that birds are easy for non-physical beings to manipulate and that many people will have visit from deceased loved ones in the form of a *winged creature. My grandmother (who is over 101) told me a couple of years back that when she passes she will give me a message from the afterlife by presenting herself as white birds. Okay, grandma, this is Tennessee. I don't know how you're going to pull that one off, but I'm watching!*

Have you ever had an experience where you just "knew" something significant was occurring and yet you couldn't explain it at the time? Linda Jones-Ellis tells about communicating telepathically with her dying co-worker who then affirmed, after his death, that he had received her message:

Ken was a handsome Rock Hudson-like gay guy whom women loved and admired. He and I worked together in the real estate business and were not all that close until I walked into the office one night and found him cleaning out his desk and packing his belongings. He was leaving the company because of a horribly rude comment a co-worker had made in which she told him people were only pretending to like him. She said that everyone knew he was gay and that no one liked him, and that they were laughing at him behind his back. I was able to help him see that this woman was lying as it was common for her to manipulate and upset people, and get them into trouble in any way she could. Ken's co-workers loved him dearly and were not talking critically of him at all. Ken was thankful for my explanation and made the decision not to leave the company.

About that time Ken had a farm listed for sale and I had a client who wanted to purchase the property. Ken and I made the 150 mile round-trip several times working on this sale. That is when we began to get to know one another, and I learned that he had AIDS. His parents refused to accept that he was gay or support him in any way. Ken's parents rejected him and all the friends and co-workers who did support him.

When Ken became too ill to care for himself, his friends at the real estate office took turns sitting with him day and night. When we received the call that Ken probably would not make it through the night, I jumped into the car with another co-worker and off we went to be with Ken in his final hours.

On the way there she asked, "What are you going to say to him?"

"If I get the chance, I'm going to ask him to let me know he's okay when he gets to the other side," I answered.

"You're NOT going to ask him that, Linda!"

"ONLY if it seems right," I replied. I was deep in thought.

When we arrived, there were so many of Ken's friends and co-workers present we had to wait in line just to get a chance to see him for ten minutes. When my turn came I took Ken's hand and looked into his eyes. Our eyes seemed locked into eternity and I didn't have to say a thing. All the love inside us merged and I just knew that everything I had wanted to say was being downloaded into him. When I left his room, I burst into tears. Ken passed a few hours later.

The next morning a Teri, a co-worker, phoned me and said, "Linda, the strangest thing happened last night and you are the only person I can tell this to who might understand."

"I got the call this morning. Ken passed last night," I said.

"I know," she said, "but he came to see me when I was in the shower last night! I was getting ready to go and sit with him for the night shift. He appeared in front of me while I was shampooing my hair." He said, 'Hi Teri!', and I said, "Ken, you look great", and he said, 'I feel great!'. Then I heard other voices saying, 'Come on Ken. If you're going with us, you have to come NOW!'"

Teri said, "At that moment my roommate walked in to tell me that she had received a call and that Ken had passed. I told her, "I know, he just came by to visit me while I was in the shower!"

I believed Teri. I knew that her experience was real. At the funeral, Teri and I were the only ones there with dry eyes. We were actually smiling!

As the days went by I frequently thought about Ken and wondered if he would let me hear from him. Late one night I was lying on my side in bed when I felt the weight of someone sitting down on the bed behind me. I panicked and wondered whether I had locked my doors before retiring. Instantly and without moving I thought, "Ken! Is that you?" The mattress moved downward the way it would if someone quickly pushed the weight of their hand on it, just behind my back. I knew that signaled "yes"!

I turned to look for him and saw a light at the foot of my bed. It was a white light, as bright as a welding torch flame and I knew in my heart it was Ken. I remembered my dad saying you shouldn't look at a welder's flame because it would damage your eyes. I hid my face in my pillow, and cried out, "Ken, I'm scared."

In that instant he was gone, but I knew with all my heart that Ken had come to let me know he was okay. Berating myself for being afraid when I had asked for contact, I continued to try to communicate to him that if he would come again I would not be afraid.

Six months later Ken came to me in a dream in which I was giving a report to some people located to my far right. Ahead of me and slightly to *my left was an open doorway where Ken appeared with his right hand in his pocket, casually leaning his left side against the door frame. He was making contact with the people to my far right and during their exchange I had an opportunity to just observe him. Slowly he turned his head, and smiling, looked straight at me. "Are you surprised to see me?" he asked sweetly.*

As my heart swelled with joy, I smiled back while shaking my head indicating "No". Then he walked forward and embraced me. Instantly I awoke from the dream, but I will never forget how it felt to connect with him again.

Our loved ones who have crossed over communicate with us in a variety of ways. They may bring a familiar smell, or leave coins, feathers or other objects in our path. They may appear as a bird, an animal or take human form. They may come to us in our dreams, or may be the voice we hear in our head. No matter how you sense their presence you can be assured that YOU'RE NOT CRAZY! They really are near and they want to communicate. Do you have ears to hear what the spirit is saying? Do you see More Than Meets the Eye?

Conclusion

Life and death are not random events; they are choices we make at a soul level. Everything that happens is in Divine order and is assisted with Divine help.

As it is in heaven so it is on earth and vice-versa. Birth, death and rebirth are simply part of a cycle similar to the seasons of our earth. There are seasons of planting, growing, waiting, harvesting, fading and resurrection. Even the time of winter or dormancy is an active time; for without it decomposition could not occur. And what is decomposition except for one thing being transformed into another? Energy replaces energy whether we see it or not. Death may seem like a dormant season, but it is far from it.

Like the proverbial glass that is both half full and half empty, a soul is both here on earth and on the other side. There are many dimensions and facets of our soul yet to be discovered. Death and life show a work in progress—a work intended to help us return to Source.

Do not be afraid! If death is upon you, rebirth is on its way. There's always a springtime to follow. We are just passing through this veil. There's always more than meets the eye!

Appendix A

A Living Will, also known as a Health Care Directive or Advanced Health Care Directive, is a legal document used to specify the healthcare or life support you would like to receive under certain conditions. If you are admitted to the hospital you will probably be asked if you have a living will. It is different from a Last Will and Testament, and does not take the place of one.

The declaration on the next page was created by an attorney and will stand as a legal document should you wish to use it. Please note that the verbiage it contains is opposed to life-sustaining procedures. If your desire is to receive life-sustaining procedures, you will need to re-word the declaration to your liking.

You will need to have two witnesses, (preferably non-relatives), to sign with you. Having the document notarized is optional. You may want to make copies of the signed document and give it to the person(s) most likely to be faced with making a healthcare decision for you should you be unable to oversee or communicate your desire.

DECLARATION

Declaration made this _____ day of
_____, 20_____.

I, _____,
being of sound mind, willfully and voluntarily make
known my desire that my dying shall not be artificially
prolonged under the circumstances set forth below and
do hereby declare:

If at any time I should have an incurable injury,
disease, or illness certified to be a terminal and
irreversible condition by two physicians who have
personally examined me, one of whom shall be my
attending physician, and the physicians have
determined that my death will occur whether or not life-
sustaining procedures are utilized and where the
application of life-sustaining procedures would serve
only to prolong artificially the dying process, I direct
that such procedures be withheld or withdrawn and that
I be permitted to die naturally with only the
administration or the performance of any medical
procedure deemed necessary to provide me with
comfort care.

In the absence of my ability to give directions
regarding the use of such life-sustaining procedures, it
is my intention that this declaration shall be honored by
my family and physician(s) as the final expression of
my legal right to refuse medical or surgical treatment
and accept the consequences from such refusal.

I understand the full import of this declaration and I am emotionally and mentally competent to make this declaration.

_____
Declarant's Signature

City:_____

County: _____ State/Province:
_____

The declarant has been personally known to me and I believe the declarant to be of sound mind.

_____
WITNESS

_____
WITNESS

(Page 2 of 2)

160

Appendix B

Warning Signs Of Suicide:

- Talk about suicide or death
- Withdrawal from family and friends
- Sudden behavioral changes
- Wanting to "tie up loose ends" or give away belongings
- Reckless behavior
- Withdrawal from regular activities
- Sudden change in sleeping patterns or eating habits

Bibliography

Abraham-Hicks article dated January 8, 2000 <u>Quarterly Journal</u>. 12 December 2004. <http://www.abraham-hicks.com/Knowledge/Abraham/Newsletters/QJ13/quotes.html>.

"Arterial Embalming." 17 January 2005. <http://search.msn.com/results.aspx?FORM=MSNH&q=embalming%20process>

Assisted Suicide Funding Restriction Act of 1997. Retrieved November 27, 2001. <http://www.oig.lsc.gov/lscpages/pl105-12.htm>.

Atwater, P.M.H. <u>We Live Forever: The Real Truth about Death.</u> Virginia: A.R.E. Press, 2004.

Atwater, P.M. H. with David H. Morgan. <u>The Complete Idiot's Guide to Near-Death Experiences</u>. Indiana: Alpha Books, 2000.

Atwater, P.M.H. Beyond the Light: The Mysteries and Revelations of Near-Death Experiences. New York: Avon Books, 1994.

Balch, Burke J. J.D., and Randall K. O'Bannon, M.A. *Why We Shouldn't Legalize Assisting Suicide*. Article in quotes. Retrieved November 29, 2001. <http://wwweuthanasia.com/index.html>.

Baskin-Jones, Michele. "An Overview of Suicide." <u>About.com Death and Dying Guide</u>. 7 January 2005.

<http://dying.about.com/cs/copingresources/a/suicide_views.htm>.

Baskin-Jones, Michele. "An Overview of World Beliefs." About.com Death and Dying Guide. 11 January 2005. <http://dying.about.com/cs/religiousviews/a/Religious_Views.htm>.

Baskin-Jones, Michele. "Signs of Dying." About.com Death and Dying Guide. 18 January 2005. <http://dying.about.com/cs/caregivers/a/DyingSigns.htm>.

Blankenship, Miranda. "Re: Jimmy's Suicide." Email. 24 September 2004.

Browne, Sylvia. Past Lives, Future Healing: A Psychic Reveals the Secrets to Good Health and Great Relationships. New York: Dutton, 2001.

Cimerian. "Walk-ins: What Are They?" Portal of Light. 11 January 2005. <http://portaloflight.org/id35.htm>.

Cooper, Anita K. "Gary Kuhn's former student." Email. 29 January 2005.

"Embalming." Quinn Peebles Funeral Home. 17 January 2005. <http://64.177.174.168/embalming.htm>.

"Embalming—The Basics of Embalming and Funeral Services." Aurora Casket Company. 17 January 2005. <http://www.funeralplan.com/products/embalming.html>.

Emge, Teri. Telephone interview. 20 December 2004.

Ettinger, Robert C.W. "Your Last Best Chance For Life--and Your Family's." Cryonics Institute. 17 January 2005. <http://www.cryonics.org/>.

Forget, Paula. Personal Interview. 22 January, 2005.

Hinman, Lawrence M. University of San Diego. MSN Encarta.
29 November 2001. <http://encarta.msn.com>.

Houser, Marsha. Personal interview. 10 September 2004.

Howser, John. "Special Report: On Death and Dying at
VUMC." Vanderbilt University Medical Center House
Organ. October 2004: 8-18.

Jones, Jan. "Alive Hospice." Windows to Wellness radio
interview conducted by Linda Woods. 17 February 2001.

Johansen, Jay. "Euthanasia: A Case of Individual Liberty?" 26
November 2001.
<http://www.pregnantpause.org/euth/index.html>.

Jones-Ellis, Linda. Telephone Interview. 21 October 2004.

Kubler-Ross, M.D., Elisabeth. *On Death and Dying.* 29
November 2001. <http://home.netcom.com/~cureltd/>.

Lindsay, David. "The Out-of-Body Experience." Spirit of
Change Magazine Online. 11 January 2005.
<http://www.spiritofchange.org/fa091004c.shtml>.

Longmire, Jennifer. "Story about your friend who died." Email.
6 December 2004.

Loyd, Faye. "Story about Catherine Smith." Email. 29
September 2004.

Manogue, Joanie. Personal interview. 15 October 2004.

Milstone, Dr. Aaron. Personal Interview. 29 December 2004.

Majors, Vickie. "Personal Stories Needed." Email. 29
November 2004.

Matson, Jake. "Story about grandmother." Email. 8 October 2004.

Moran, Lisa. "Story about Randy". Email. 10 January 2005.

Mueller, Tommy. Personal Interview. 9 November 2004.

Myers, Kathy. "Dealing with the Dying." Christian Medical Fellowship. 20 November 2004. < http://www.cmf.org.uk/index.htm?nucleus/nucapr00/dying.htm>.

Nightingale, Rev. Juliet. "The Near-Death Experience." Toward The Light. 29 October 2004. <http://www.towardthelight.org/pages/2/index.htm>.

Norris, Kaye and Gretchen Strohmaier, Drs. Charles & Ira Byock. "Spiritual Care at the End of Life: Some Clergy Lack Training in End-of-Life Care." Health Progress. July-Aug 2004 issue. 5 January 2005. <http://www.dyingwell.org/spiritualcarehp0704.htm>.

Parrish, Charlotte. "Suicide Toll Tops Murder in Tennessee." The News Herald. 21 October 2004: 1, 4.

Partnership for Caring. 28 November 2001. <http://www.partnershipforcaring.org/Talking/talking_set.html>.

Perry, Randy. Personal interview. 12 October 2004.

Prophet, Elizabeth Clare. Reincarnation: The Missing Link in Christianity. Montana: Summit University Press, 1997.

Roth, Tammy. Personal interview. 7 October 2004.

"The American Journal of Psychiatry." 1986. Retrieved November 27, 2001. <http://www.law.cornell.edu/lii.html>.

The International Association for Near-Death Studies, Inc. 20 November 2004. <http://www.iands.org/>.

"The UTHSCSA Willed Body Program: Benefiting Future Generations Through the Gift of Your Body." The University of North Texas Health Science at San Antonio. 17 January 2005.<http://www.uthscsa.edu/csb/willedbody/>

"The Willed Body Program." The University of North Texas Health Science at Fort Worth. 17 January 2005. <http://www.hsc.unt.edu/departments/pathology_anatomy/willedbody/faq.htm#q1>

Uhlmann, Michael M. Legal Logic of Euthanasia. 29 November 2001. <http://supct.law.cornell.edu/cgi-bin/sup-choice.cgi?197+11>.

Villoldo, Alberto. Shaman, Sage, Healer: How to Heal Yourself and Others with the Energy Medicine of the Americas. New York: Harmony Books, 2000.

Virtue, Doreen. Karma Releasing Clearing Away Painful Patterns From Your Past. Hay House, 1999.

"What You Should Know about Embalming." Funeral Consumers Alliance. 17 January 2005. <http://www.funerals.org/faq/embalm.htm>.

Womack, Mary Anne. "Crossover." Email. 27 September 2004.

Woods, Linda. "Your Story about Irving." Email. 28 November 2004.

Wray, Mark. Personal interview. 4 January 2005.